THURBER, TEXAS

THE LIFE AND DEATH OF A COMPANY COAL TOWN

John S. Spratt, Sr.
Edited by Harwood P. Hinton
Foreword by T. Lindsay Baker

Nov 30, 1936

Dear Jackie!,
 Keep this card The
postmark is the last one from
Thurber. It might be valuable
someday. The Thurber Office
closes today.
                Love, Geneva Spratt

THIS SIDE OF CARD IS FOR ADDRESS

THURBER
NOV
30
5 PM
1936
TEX.

Jack Spratt Jr.
San Angelo,
Box 324.   Texas

THURBER, TEXAS

THE LIFE AND DEATH OF A COMPANY COAL TOWN

John S. Spratt, Sr.
Edited by Harwood P. Hinton
Foreword by T. Lindsay Baker

State✦House
Press
McMurry University
Abilene, Texas

First Edition Cloth, 1986
First Edition Paper, 2005

Requests for permission to reproduce material from this work should be
sent to State House Press, McMurry Station, Box 637, Abilene, Texas
79697-0637.

Library of Congress Cataloging-in-Publication Data

Spratt, John S. (John Stricklin), 1902-1976.
    Thurber, Texas: the life and death of a company coal town.

    (Personal narratives of the West series)
    Bibliography: p.
    Includes index.
    1. Spratt, John S. (John Stricklin), 1902-1976. 2. Thurber (Tex.)—
Biography. 3. Thurber Region (Tex.)—Social life and customs. 4. Coal
mines and mining—Texas—Thurber Region—History—20th century.
IHinton, Harwood P., 1927- . II. Title. III. Series

F394.T48S67   1986   976.4'551   85.22570
ISBN-13: 978-1-933337-00-5
ISBN-10: 1-933337-00-1

Distributed by Texas A&M University Press Consortium
(800) 826-8911 • www.tamu.edu/upress

Cover designed by Rosenbohm Graphic Design

ISBN 1-933337-00-1 paper

10 9 8 7 6 5 4 3 2 1

(Frontispiece) Last piece of mail from Thurber post office,
November 30, 1936. Courtesy J.S. Spratt, Jr.

Contents

Acknowledgments

I N EDITING this manuscript and locating appropriate illustrations, I have incurred numerous debts. The following checked historical data for me: Ralph Elder, Barker Center, University of Texas at Austin; Mary A. Sarber, El Paso Public Library; Michael Q. Hooks, Southwest Collection, Texas Tech University, Lubbock; and the staffs of the Fort Worth Public Library and University of Arizona Library. Jo Felts, Cody, Wyoming; Ola Lou Spratt Smith, Fairfield, California; and Geneva Spratt, Mineral Wells, Texas, supplied numerous Spratt family materials. George Batik, Department of Biomedical Communications and Photography, University of Louisville, School of Medicine, Louisville, Kentucky, provided several expert reproductions for the volume.

Special thanks go to John S. Spratt, Jr., his mother, Nan Spratt, and his brother, Thomas Spratt, who encouraged me to undertake this project. The Jack Spratt family have been dear friends since my college days, and I was greatly honored to be asked to edit Jack's memoir for publication. I hope that both family and friends will be pleased with my effort.

H.P.H.

Foreword

For many years Texas-born Harwood P. Hinton taught state and regional history and edited the award-winning history quarterly, *Arizona and the West*, at the University of Arizona, Tucson, but he remained tied to the Lone Star State. During the 1930s as a youth he made many trips to visit relatives living at or near Thurber in Erath County. Even during his long tenure as a history professor in Arizona, he conducted research on pioneer Texas ranchers. At his retirement he returned to Texas and served as one of the senior editors for the six-volume *New Handbook of Texas*.

Hinton returned to Texas in one more way—and that was to edit portions of a huge manuscript written by Dr. John S. Spratt, Sr., an economics professor at Southern Methodist University, who grew up in Mingus, three miles from Thurber. Hinton had known the Spratt family of Mingus from his childhood visits and later became a close friend with John S. Spratt, Jr., while a student at the University of Texas at Austin. From the much larger manuscript, Hinton extracted the parts that dealt with daily life in Mingus and in the nearby coal-mining town of Thurber for this book.

In 1881 Mingus came into existence on the main line of the Texas and Pacific Railroad, and it drew its life from the busy traffic on its steel rails. Older than Thurber, it also outlived the coal town just three miles to its south. Thurber, though having four times the population of Mingus, depended on the smaller community as its essential rail link with the outside world. Miners could extract bituminous coal from beneath Thurber because the railroad carried it to buyers elsewhere. By the same token, the rail link made possible the second industry of Thurber—brick making, initiated in 1897. Heavy and bulky bricks could be shipped economically only by trains, and the steel rails running north from Thurber carried regular shipments to the main line at Mingus and distant markets.

In his memoir John Spratt clearly delineates both the similarities and differences between the mostly Anglo railroad town of Mingus and the highly diverse company-owned coal-mining town of Thurber. The remembrance could come only from one who lived during the heyday of the two communities. We are fortunate that Spratt grew up in Mingus and that he later became a scholar who realized the importance of recording the events of his childhood.

Thanks to John S. Spratt, Sr., we have an insider's view of life in industrial Texas during the early twentieth century. Pick up this book, read through its pages, and take a trip on a mental time machine to the days when Thurber produced tons of coal every day—and saw all of it pass by rail to Mingus and onto the main line to reach buyers. Join John Spratt by reading these pages, and through his eyes view a part of Texas that once boomed, then languished, and vanished into obscurity. This is a gem of Texas industrial history.

T. Lindsay Baker
Director, W. K. Gordon Center for
Industrial History of Texas, Thurber

Introduction

J ACK SPRATT long remembered the shrill sound of train whistles
and the sight of coal soot that covered his front porch every
morning. The Spratt home sat about one hundred yards north
of the main line of the Texas & Pacific Railroad in the hamlet of
Mingus, a rail junction snuggled in the hilly farming country west of
Fort Worth. Daily life in Mingus revolved around the coming and
going of passenger and freight trains. And each workday switch engines chugged into town from the south, pulling gondola cars loaded
with coal from the booming Thurber mines. Great clouds of black
dust rose into the air when the gondolas dumped their contents into
coal chutes to feed the hungry T&P locomotives that regularly sped
west and east over ribbons of steel to distant points. In his youth,
Spratt became fascinàted with the world about him and, toward the
end of a long career in teaching, he recorded his recollections of this
unique industrial setting. The result is a colorful chapter in Texas
history.[1]

In 1900 Texas was booming. An expanding network of railroads
had transformed the economy of the state from one of small shops
and subsistence farming to one of manufacturing and intensive agriculture. The iron horse had spurred the rise of new industries, encouraged a shift to money crops such as cotton, and shortened the
distance between producer and consumer. One industry that profited
from the boom was coal. As locomotives consumed large amounts of
this fuel, the development of mines was critical to economic expan-
sion. The most famous coal district in Texas during these years was
at Thurber, owned by the Texas & Pacific Coal Company (no kin to
the railroad).[2]

The origins of Thurber were intimately tied to the building of the
Texas & Pacific Railroad. Surveying crews pushing west in the late
1870s reported a coal outcropping in the cedar-studded hills in southern Palo Pinto County. This was part of a low-to-medium grade bi-

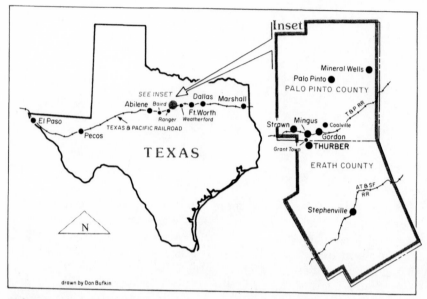

Palo Pinto and Erath counties

tuminous belt that extended from Wise County, north of Fort Worth, southwest to Coleman County. In the late summer of 1880, as railroad work trains approached the hamlet of Gordon, named for T&P engineer H. L. Gordon, several businessmen opened a drift mine on the west side of Clayton Mountain, some three miles northeast of the town. James, Cowan & Nolton Company, owners of the mine, hired a local labor force and contracted to furnish coal to the T&P.[3]

The mine near Gordon was the first commercial coal operation in Texas. From Coalville, as the site was called, wagons rumbled down the mountain and dumped chunks of the black fuel at the rail siding. As its track crews proceeded west, the T&P bought the mine and laid a spur to the site. Other shafts were opened and Coalville grew and soon boasted the largest school in the county. Here also the Knights of Labor, a national industrial union, organized its first miners' local in Texas. In April of 1884 the Knights called a strike, but the T&P ignored their demands and, as the quality of the coal was poor, abandoned the mines. Some workers returned to their farms while others sought employment in neighboring districts.[4]

A number of miners found jobs at the Johnson coal mine in Erath County, a few miles to the southwest. William W. Johnson, a former civil engineer, had settled at the neighboring town of Strawn and contracted to provide cross ties and cedar posts to the railroad. In the fall of 1886, with his brother Harvey, he opened a coal mine in a basin two miles south of the main T&P track and obtained a contract to furnish fuel to the railroad. Dozens of tents and shacks soon dotted the area. The Knights quickly became active here, too, and in 1887 won concessions for the workers. But the Johnsons plunged into debt for new enterprises, became entangled in managerial difficulties, and failed to meet their payrolls. The miners struck and the mine was closed.[5]

In early fall of 1888 a group of investors organized the Texas & Pacific Coal Company and purchased the Johnson interests in Erath and Palo Pinto counties. The new owners included Robert D. Hunter, a millionaire cattle broker, his son-in-law Edgar L. Marston, H. K. Thurber of New York, and a group of Eastern capitalists. Hunter, a tough businessman, was president and general manager of the new company. He visited the idled coal mine and announced plans to start production. He would put the miners back to work if they would cut their ties with the Knights and accept reduced pay. Those unwilling to work on these terms were ordered to vacate the property. To enforce his rules, Hunter built a fence around the coal camp, installed gates, and in time hired guards to patrol the line on horseback. The company renegotiated the coal contract with the T&P Railroad, which laid track from its main line into the valley.[6]

When the Knights urged the miners to resist, Hunter called on the governor's office for help, and ten Texas Rangers were assigned in December of 1888 to keep order in the district. At the same time, Hunter asked Marston to hire strikebreakers and replacement workers in the East. On January 2, 1889, the camp was officially named Thurber, after one of the company stockholders. Scabs and immigrant labor soon began rolling in from the coal mines of Pennsylvania and the Midwest. By winter, the Knights, sensing their cause was futile, called off the strike, and peace returned to the district.[7]

Thurber grew during the 1890s. New mines were opened in the hills west of town (eventually there would be fourteen shafts in operation). Thurber developed as a company town. A subsidiary corporation, the Texas & Pacific Mercantile and Manufacturing Company, was created to manage the company's business enterprises. These included stores, saloons, ice and power plant, schools, churches, opera house, boarding houses, dairy, newspaper and printing shop, and dwellings. Hunter hired W. K. Gordon, a personable young engineer from Virginia, to manage his fiefdom. Foreign-born workers in the Thurber mines significantly increased during the nineties, with nearly one thousand arriving by 1900. Approximately one-half of them were Italian; the rest were English, German, Austrian, Irish, Polish, and black. Families congregated on the hills surrounding the basin, and soon there was an Italian Hill, Stump Hill, Polander Hill, and so on. The population in and around Thurber in 1900 exceeded three thousand.[8]

As in every mining camp, liquor became an important issue. After Hunter built his fence, he sought to drive out Jimmy Grant, who was running a saloon nearby. This prompted Grant to move his establishment north across the line into Palo Pinto County, three-quarters of a mile from Thurber. Here a small settlement called Grant Town sprang up. To profit from booming liquor sales, Hunter promptly built several company-owned saloons in Thurber. After Erath County voted to go dry in 1904, the company opened a large drinking emporium, dubbed the Snake, across the line in Palo Pinto County. Its large horseshoe bar could serve several hundred customers at a time.[9]

In February of 1897, R. D. Hunter joined James Green of St. Louis in establishing the Green & Hunter Brick Company at Thurber. The T&P properties contained large deposits of shale, and Hunter reckoned that discarded pea coal could be used for firing brick kilns. He erected a plant in the southeast part of town and laid rail lines to shale beds in the adjoining hills. By fall the new enterprise was producing dry-pressed bricks in the most modern facility west of the Mississippi River. Profits soared as Thurber brick found ready markets in the Southwest for buildings, streets, highways, and heavy construction. The Galveston Sea Wall was built of Thurber brick, as was Congress Avenue in the capital, Austin.[10]

Hunter retired from control of the coal and brick companies in 1899, and Edgar Marston became president. Marston soon faced a major challenge. The United Mine Workers had become active in Texas and now focused their attention on Thurber. At first, company guards grabbed union organizers and escorted them outside the "wire," but representatives from the neighboring unionized mines at Lyra and Strawn filtered in and found support. Company manager W. K. Gordon tried to stave off unionization. He rejected both pay demands and UMW recognition and obtained a small company of Texas Rangers to keep order and protect property. As a crisis approached in 1903, company president Marston came from New York and met with strike leaders. After extended talks he decided to recognize the union. By 1907 Thurber, a town with fourteen hundred men on the payroll, became one of the first totally union towns in the nation. The coal district entered its most prosperous years.[11]

* * *

Thurber was booming when Dr. John Thomas Spratt moved his family from West Texas to Thurber Junction (Mingus) in 1904.

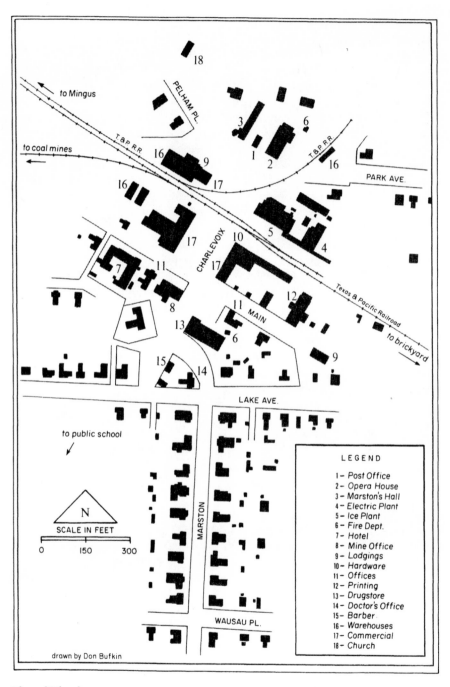

Plat of Thurber

Mingus was small in contrast to its industrial neighbor to the south. It had a depot, switching yards, coal chutes, a few stores, and fewer than two thousand people, most of whom worked for the railroad or served passenger and freight traffic. Spratt purchased four acres just north of the depot and built a house and office. The inhabitants of Mingus were principally from neighboring farms and composed an entirely different ethnic stock from the mixed nationalities working in the Thurber mines. They were primarily Anglo-Saxon frontier folk with attitudes and values rooted deeply in the soil. As Thurber grew, many of them saw a lucrative market there for farm products, but the T&P Company, seeking to create and control its own source of supply, discouraged outsiders from peddling or selling foodstuffs there. Mingus, however, provided a small, but steady market for home-grown products.[12]

The Spratt family fitted easily into local society. John T. Spratt had been born in Nelsonville, Missouri, on September 5, 1875, grew up on a farm, and in his youth moved to Erath County, Texas. He entered the Dallas Medical School (forerunner of Baylor Medical), cut wood to pay for his education, and graduated first in his class in 1902. In the meantime he had married Louisa Felts at Huckaby, Erath County, and on receiving his medical degree, they left for Pecos in West Texas. (Louisa's sister Callie was married to Bill Ross, a prominent rancher, who had helped finance John's education.) After two years of general practice, Spratt sought a more desirable climate and better career prospects. He moved his family to Mingus. As the only doctor in town, Spratt added class and quality to the community. A tall, dapper young man who was friendly and ambitious, he quickly built a thriving practice and in time opened a drugstore and pharmacy there.[13]

John Stricklin Spratt, the author of the memoir that follows, grew up in the Thurber district during its boom years. He was born July 5, 1902, in Pecos and early developed a curiosity for the events and folk around him. He soaked up stories of a rural past rapidly fading from memory and took a warm delight in the company of his grandfather Kindred S. Felts, a Confederate veteran, in the characters who frequented the center of town—the depot—and in the special events in Thurber that his family attended. Life in Mingus centered on the railroad. Passing trains brought circuses, soldiers (during the war years), traveling salesmen, politicians, and weekly carloads of beer from Fort Worth for the thirsty miners. Although only one-fourth the size of Thurber, the town enjoyed a ready access to the mainstream of American life.[14]

Jack attended primary schools in Mingus, attended high school for two years in neighboring Strawn, then rode the train east each week to Weatherford to complete his work. As a senior, Jack (dubbed "High Pockets") managed the high school football team, served on the debate team, and edited the yearbook. He entered the University of Texas at Austin in 1920 and became active in campus politics, but dropped out to teach school for several years. In 1927 he married Nannie Lee Morgan in Ranger, and the following year obtained a bachelor's and master's degree in history at Texas. He took a position at San Angelo College in West Texas, where he headed the Department of Social Sciences from 1928 to 1943, and served as associate editor of the *South-Western Sheep and Goat Raiser* journal. Spratt joined the economics faculty at Southern Methodist University in 1946, and completed the Ph.D. seven years later at the University of Texas. A tall, thin man with a ready smile, a great sense of humor, and a gruff voice, he now entered the most productive years of his career.[15]

In March of 1956 Jack Spratt won the Carr P. Collins Award, given by the prestigious Texas Institute of Letters, for *The Road to Spindletop: Economic Change in Texas, 1875–1901*, an outgrowth of his doctoral dissertation. In this volume, adjudged "the best Texas book of the year" in 1955, Spratt analyzed and described the economic forces that provided the basis for Texas's recovery after the troubled days of Reconstruction and set the stage for the industrial boom that followed the blowing in of the Lucas gusher in the Spindletop field at Beaumont. Spratt planned a second volume and after his retirement from Southern Methodist University in 1967, he devoted full time to the project.[16]

In studying the early years of the twentieth century, Spratt became increasingly aware of the unique world he had known in the Mingus-Thurber area. He had seen firsthand the influence of the T&P Railroad on life in the coal district and on the chain of events that sent Thurber into decline after 1917 and precipitated the demise of his hometown of Mingus. A student of economics, he also understood the role that management, technology, and progress played in hastening the destruction of the two communities. Here was a case study that vividly reflected a significant aspect of the change in the Texas economy after 1900.

In the late 1960s Spratt went back to Mingus and Thurber, talked to old-timers, walked familiar streets, and sought out sites of memorable events. The ranks of the pioneer families had thinned (his father had died in 1958), but he was encouraged in his work and eventually composed a lengthy manuscript. In this work, he described his youth, commented on economic changes since 1900, and ventured predictions. As he redrafted parts of it, the thrust of the story gradually shifted toward a memoir. Unfortunately, he was unable to complete his project because of ill health. John S. Spratt died in Dallas on July 16, 1976, of cancer.[17]

The edited version that follows focuses on Jack Spratt's youth, from about 1906 to 1920. In these pages, Spratt vividly recalls the world that was Thurber. He describes the operation of the mines, the local business scene in Thurber and Mingus, and the various celebrations and events that added color and gaiety to the coal mining center. He also writes in some detail about his family life, school experiences, pastimes, and chores. Spratt was a perceptive observer, and his personal account affords a classic commentary on the history of the Thurber district. I have annotated the text as necessary to interpret or explain certain references.

This is Jack Spratt's story. For those who knew Thurber and Mingus in bygone days, he provides a memorable nostalgia trip. For those who travel Interstate 20 and wonder about the ruins languishing in the valley a few miles east of Ranger Hill, here is an explanation. Steam engines no longer snort and pound, the whistles are stilled, and the coal soot is gone, but the personality and significance of this picturesque world live on in these valuable recollections.

Tucson, Arizona   HARWOOD P. HINTON

---

[1] For more information on Thurber, see Michael Q. Hooks, "Thurber: A Unique Texas Community," *Panhandle-Plains Historical Review* 56 (1983): 1–17; Mary Jane Gentry, "Thurber, Life and Death of a Texas Town" (M.A. thesis, University of Texas, 1946); Weldon B. Hardman, *Fire in a Hole*. Hardman's is a general account of the Thurber coal district based on information drawn from old-time residents. Also see Gordon Gooch, "Mingus, the Pittsburgh of Texas," *Junior Historian* 13 (May 1953): 6; and Leo S. Bielinski, "Beer, Booze, Bootlegging and Bocci Ball in Thurber-Mingus," *West Texas Historical Association Year Book* 59 (1983): 75–89; John N. Cravens, "Two Miners and Their Families in the Thurber-Strawn Coal Mines, 1905–1918," *West Texas Historical Association Year Book* 45 (1969): 115–126.

[2] John S. Spratt, *The Road to Spindletop: Economic Change in Texas, 1875–1901*; Rupert N. Richardson et al., *Texas: The Lone Star State*, chap. 14.

[3] Walter P. Webb, ed., *Handbook of Texas*, I, 366, 711; Gentry, "Thurber," pp. 1–6; Hardman, *Fire*, pp. 7–10.

[4] Gentry, "Thurber," pp. 6–7, 49; Hardman, *Fire*, pp. 8–11; Ruth Allen, *Chapters in the History of Organized Labor in Texas*, pp. 91, 104; Spratt, *Road*, p. 263.

⁵Gentry, "Thurber," pp. 7–8; Allen, *Chapters*, pp. 91–92; Hardman, *Fire*, pp. 13–14, 23–26; Hooks, "Thurber," pp. 1–2.

⁶Allen, *Chapters*, pp. 92, 94, 96, 104–105, 107. The T&P Coal Company also acquired twenty thousand acres adjoining the coal district: Gentry, "Thurber," pp. 9–14; Hardman, *Fire*, pp. 15–18, 25–28, 33, 90; Hooks, "Thurber," p. 3; *Abilene Reporter-News*, September 4, 1966; *Fort Worth Star-Telegram*, August 13, 1975.

⁷Allen, *Chapters*, pp. 92–93, 96, 102–106; Hardman, *Fire*, pp. 29–31, 34.

⁸Sixteen shafts were opened in the Thurber district, but the last (1917) was never developed: Allen, *Chapters*, pp. 94, 96, 101, 106–109; Gentry, "Thurber," pp. 95, 105–121, 135, 185. Buckley B. Paddock, *History of Texas: Fort Worth and the Texas Northwest Edition*, II, 554–558, gives a short history of Thurber. Hardman, *Fire*, pp. 19–22, 63–64, 89–90, 101, 127–131, explains that only fourteen of the sixteen numbered shafts (there was no No. 13 and No. 16 was never worked) were in regular operation. Also see Hooks, "Thurber," pp. 4–10, which provides factual information on the district's beginnings.

⁹Gentry, "Thurber," pp. 71, 99, 128; Hardman, *Fire*, pp. 33, 95; Hooks, "Thurber," p. 13.

¹⁰Gentry, "Thurber," pp. 42–44; Paddock, *Fort Worth*, II, 555; Hardman, *Fire*, chap. 7.

¹¹James C. Maroney, "The Unionization of Thurber, 1903," *Red River Valley Historical Review* 4 (Spring 1979): 27–32; Allen, *Chapters*, pp. 96–98, 110–117; Gentry, "Thurber," pp. 77–95; Hardman, *Fire*, chap. 5; Webb, *Handbook of Texas*, I, 710–711; Hooks, "Thurber," pp. 14–15.

¹²Webb, *Handbook of Texas*, II, 213; Hardman, *Fire*, pp. 90–91; *Dallas Morning News*, September 4, 1958; tax receipts and notes, John S. Spratt, Sr., Collection.

¹³Spratt Notes, Spratt Collection; see *Abilene Reporter-News*, *Dallas Morning News*, *Fort Worth Star-Telegram* for September 4, 1958.

¹⁴Spratt Notes, Spratt Collection.

¹⁵Spratt Notes and school annuals, Spratt Collection.

¹⁶*San Angelo Standard-Times*, March 12, 1956; *Mustang* (Southern Methodist University), May 1956, p. 25; and undated clippings in Spratt Collection.

¹⁷John S. Spratt, Sr., to Harwood P. Hinton, January 22, 1976, editor's files.

Preface

THE TOWN of Thurber, located seventy miles west of Fort Worth, Texas, was the center of a booming coal mining district for nearly thirty years. Together with Mingus, only two miles away, it was the most important industrial unit between Fort Worth and El Paso until the early 1920s. Demand for coal by the Texas & Pacific Railway Company was responsible for creating the two towns. Thurber was the base of operations for fourteen mines, and Mingus was the shipping point and service center for the railroad cars that regularly distributed coal along the T&P's main line. Bound to one resource, the two communities grew in importance as the demand for coal increased—then died slow deaths when the T&P converted its locomotives into oil burners. By 1935 there was no Thurber, and Mingus had shrunk to a small and insignificant village. Both were victims of the creative process of building a new America.

Although inextricably tied by coal, each town was quite different in origin and character. Thurber was built and wholly owned by the Texas & Pacific Coal Company. All the residents worked for the company and at one time were even required to live in town. Some twenty different nationalities composed a majority of the labor force that worked the mines. Mingus, on the other hand, was a village comprising individual proprietorships, the only corporate properties being the railroad shops, coal chutes, and depot. The contrast in property ownership was vividly reflected in how people worked and lived in each town.

My father, Dr. John Thomas Spratt, moved the family to Mingus in 1904, when, as a rancher would say, I was a coming two-year-old. Here I grew up while he practiced medicine. At the time there was no better place for a boy to observe one world evolve into another than being near a transcontinental line. Everything moved by rail and the panorama changed constantly. Although Thurber advanced into the twentieth century, Mingus still adhered to modes of rural life. The surrounding countryside was made up of small farms, largely self-contained, that were operated by man and beast.

In my youth, local travel was by horseback, buggy, or wagon. Fuel for heating or cooking came from wood or coal, and coal oil (kerosene) was used in family and store lamps. Organs outnumbered pianos, but fiddles were more numerous than both. A few families owned hand-cranked phonographs. Pictures viewed through stereoscopes provided hours of entertainment, as we studied the same scenes over and over. Now and then a traveling showman rented the local Woodmen of the World lodge room for a magic lantern show. The first automobile I recall was owned by John Kern around 1908, and an airplane finally appeared locally in 1911.

Semibarter was still a common practice in the Mingus-Thurber area. For many years, fully half of my father's medical fees were settled in goods. Bank checks were virtually unknown. Self-contained agriculture occupied a place of major importance, and each summer farmers drove door to door about town, selling surplus produce. The rural influence was still pervasive in Mingus, for most of the residents had come directly from the farm and annually supplemented their cash income from backyard gardens, hogpens, poultry, and milk cows. My father practiced medicine for years on horseback with a pair of medicine bags thrown across his saddle. They were filled with vials of powders and pills, from which he concocted or doled out prescribed dosages.

Thurber was the focus of our world. It boasted a large power and ice plant and had a water system that provided yard faucets to homes. However, the company-owned residences had little space for gardens and livestock other than a horse. The locomotives that shuttled coal between Thurber and Mingus were little more than toys. On the main line through Mingus, freight and passenger cars were of wooden construction. A freight train of thirty cars was something to talk about for a week. Passenger trains averaged about twenty miles per hour and freight trains ran considerably slower.

When I went off to college in 1920, many changes had taken place in the Thurber district. My father now made his rounds in a Ford coupe. The local farms, which had produced practically everything a family consumed, were rapidly shifting to specialized crops. In 1917 the T&P Coal Company brought in the Ranger oil field, and the company jumped overnight from a $3 million to a $150 million corporation. As the T&P converted its locomotives to oil, Thurber's days as a coal town were numbered. Mingus, its economic satellite, faced economic oblivion, too.

The changes taking place in Thurber and Mingus represented a pattern throughout Texas—and to some extent the whole of the United States. It was a fascinating time in which to live, a period that saw the end of the frontier and the coming of the modern age.

My primary objective in presenting these recollections is to portray the way of life in the early 1900s in Thurber and Mingus and to describe the dramatic changes that carried these two towns to their peaks of industrial significance, then destroyed one and left the other a shadow of its former self. Throughout the manuscript I have used dates, and a few of them may not be precise. As I have been primarily concerned with the panorama of change, the imprecision should in no way impair that objective.

Credit for writing this book must be given to my former graduate students. It would never have been undertaken had it not been for their prodding.

Dallas, Texas   JOHN S. SPRATT, SR.

THURBER, TEXAS

1.   From Pecos to Mingus

W E MOVED to Mingus in 1904 because my father disliked the desertlike region of West Texas. He had grown up near Nelsonville, Missouri, thirty miles west of Hannibal, on a family farm of about two hundred acres and probably would have stayed there had it not been for a bit of teenage foolishness. One day he and a bunch of boys were trying to see who could outdo the others at riding a mule backwards. My father either fell or was thrown from the mule and broke his ankle. The break was poorly set, healed in a bow shape, and caused him pain for the rest of his life. Unable to farm with a walking plow, he left Missouri and joined relatives living near Lingleville in Erath County, Texas. Finding farming just as arduous in Texas as it was in Missouri, he decided to study medicine and become a doctor.

Dad enrolled in the Fort Worth University Medical School in 1898. He had saved money from chopping wood at fifty cents a cord (he could average four cords a day) and working in the harvest fields and felt that he could earn more at Christmas breaks and during the five months of the year when school was not in session. He wrote his father that costs for medical school at Fort Worth were $76.00 for tuition, $25.00 for books, board and room at $11.00 per month, with total costs not to exceed $300.00 per school year. In his third year, Dad transferred to the Dallas Medical College, a branch of Trinity University, and there obtained his medical degree on April 15, 1902, receiving an award for the highest standing in his class. While still in school, he married Martha Louisa Felts,* whose family lived in Erath County.

---

*Martha Louisa Felts (August 4, 1881–February 15, 1965), Spratt Notes, Spratt Collection.—Ed.

John Thomas and Louisa Spratt decided to settle in Pecos, Texas. Louisa's brother-in-law, William L. Ross, a well-to-do Pecos rancher, had turned over his checkbook to Dad in his senior year, with instructions to use it for whatever he needed to finish school. He could repay the loan later. The Spratts reached Pecos in May of 1902.

Pecos had about one thousand people, and was the county seat of Reeves County. The local population was made up of ranch families, a few blacks, and a large number of Mexicans. The Mexicans lived in small adobe or crude frame huts. Most of the women worked as house servants and the men as ranch hands. Two railroads intersected at Pecos, the Texas & Pacific, running east and west, and the Santa Fe, going north.*

Dad went into a partnership with an older doctor which lasted six months.† The two differed sharply over diagnosis and treatment of patients. As there were no opportunities in Texas for postgraduate enlightenment, his erstwhile partner in October 1902 left for New York for additional graduate work and the partnership ended.

Writing to his father, Charles H. Spratt,** back in Missouri, on June 22, 1902, John Thomas said that he had taken in four hundred dollars the previous month. He had a nice office, microscope, nebulizer compressed-air outfit, and planned to buy an X-ray machine in the next few months. He would then "be fixed and prepared to do anything." He and fellow physician Jim Camp had operated on two men for appendicitis a few weeks before and "both had got well." The Pecos country was full of wild game, and he invited his father to come out for a wild boar hunt. Deer and antelope also were plentiful.

The practice of medicine was not easy in those days. Dad treated most of his patients in his office, where he also did minor operations. He performed major operations in the home and delivered babies there, too. If he made a house call in town, he walked. For out-of-town calls, Dad went by buggy, if the distance was not over a mile or

---

*This segment of the Santa Fe was originally built by the Pecos River Railroad Company in 1890–1891 from Pecos, Texas, to Eddy (Carlsbad), New Mexico, and was acquired, with extensions, by the Santa Fe in 1900 (S. G. Reed, *A History of Texas Railroads . . .* , p. 302.—Ed.

†The name of the "older doctor" is not known. John T. Spratt and Jim Camp (1877–1964) both took up practice in Pecos in 1900. Other physicians there from 1900 to 1904 were W. McKinney and a man named White (Alton Hughes, *Pecos, a History of the Pioneer West*, pp. 91, 268, 357; I. J. Bush, *Gringo Doctor*, pp. 60–61, 94, 103).—Ed.

**The family letters mentioned here and later are in the Spratt Collection.—Ed.

so. If farther, he rode horseback with medicines and basic instruments stowed in saddlebags.

In one instance, Dad made a trip in midwinter to New Mexico to see a cowhand who had the measles. A cowboy had ridden 15 miles across the mountains to the railroad and sent a telegram asking Dad to come. A blizzard was raging, and the cowhand had gotten lost, hobbled his horse, and spent the night walking the animal to keep from freezing. Reaching the railroad the following day, he wired my father to catch the mixed train for New Mexico at 3:00 P.M. After a train trip of 55 miles, Dad and the hand rode through 15 miles of snow to reach the patient. For this 140-mile trip he received a fee of some twenty-five dollars.

Writing in June of 1903 to his father in Missouri, Dad looked back on his first year of practice. He had rented a five-room house for $15.00 a month, but had let out two rooms for $12.00. This left his net rent at $3.00. He kept a cow and a pony, in addition to a pig and chickens. Feed grain cost $1.40 per hundred pounds. His medical fees averaged from $200.00 to $550.00 per month, but cash receipts produced only about $100.00 per month. Out of this income, he had just about paid Bill Ross the $500.00 he owed him for the medical school loan.

Dad's practice expanded, but he developed a dislike for Pecos. On October 24, 1903, he wrote home: "I have been by myself one year the *1st* Nov. [H]ave done $4000.00 worth of work[.] [M]y collections run about $2000.00 cash. [T]hat does mighty well I think for a beginner . . ." Yet he was dissatisfied. The stamp of the Old West was still on the land: ". . . do you recollect the man that had the Black wolf, snakes & wild animals when you were here," Dad asked, "a man by the name of Pratt killed him on the 9th Sep. [R]ode up behind him and shot him in the back with a rifle & shot him again after he fell. . . . There has been six men murdered in the county in the last six months & four of them in town . . ."

The surrounding country was a desert. Glittering alkali flats made him squint-eyed. Greasewood, mesquite, salt cedars, prairie dog towns, coyotes, rattlesnakes, plus broiling summer days, contrasted sharply with his verdant and forested native home state of Missouri. Quite to the contrary, Mother loved everything about the Trans-Pecos region. After two years, the young doctor decided to seek a new location. He had heard of the booming coal district at Thurber, three hundred miles east of Pecos, and thought that it might be a good place to settle.

During late April of 1904, Dad made arrangements to move. He chartered a boxcar from the Texas & Pacific Railway, loaded household goods, office equipment, and clothing in the back half of the car, and placed the horse, cow, buggy, saddle, harness, and feed and water for the livestock in the front. He made a place for himself in the middle section to ride as a free passenger. Here he had a chair, bed, food, and water. A freight train hooked on to the boxcar and Dad headed east.

Two or three days after leaving Pecos, the train stopped at Thurber Junction (Mingus) for coaling and to permit the crew to eat. Dad was three miles west of his destination, the town of Gordon. A brakeman said they would be there for at least thirty-five minutes, so he crawled down from the boxcar to walk around a bit to break the tedium of confinement. There was much more activity about him than he had seen at any station since leaving Pecos. Two or three switch engines were busily shunting cars, most of them loaded with coal, from track to track in the yards. The freight agent and his helpers were loading and unloading cars along a long platform. Draymen with their wagons and teams were busy with incoming and outgoing shipments.

The doctor began to ask questions about the place, conversing with members of the train crew and 3 or 4 local residents. He was told that Thurber was heading toward a population of 10,000! At Mingus the T&P Railroad employed some 150 men, while at Thurber, two miles distant, nearly 2,000 men worked in the mines owned by the Texas & Pacific Coal Company. Coal shipments and freight at Mingus were large enough to keep three to five switch engines busy around the clock.

But the information that kept Dad from traveling three miles farther east to Gordon was word that Mingus had only one doctor, an old man who might die or give up his practice at any time. On making inquiries, Dad found that he could rent a ten-by-twenty-foot unpainted frame shack right next to the post office for three dollars a month. Down the street, a block east of the depot, and north of the tracks, was a vacant three-room frame house whose owner asked ten dollars a month for it. Dad decided to stay. He had the boxcar moved onto a siding and hired drayman John T. Dyer to move the contents to the two buildings. The date was May 1, 1904.

Within the next two weeks, my father sent for Mother and me. Since we were not permitted to deadhead east in the freight car with him, we had remained in Pecos with Mother's sister, Callie Ross. From what I learned in later years, the news that Thurber Junction, not Gordon, would be our home came as quite a shock. Mother said that on arrival at Thurber Junction, she started bawling and bawled for the remainder of the day. She never stopped hating what she called "that damned place."

Mother had been reared on an Erath County farm and knew that farmers were good people. Pecos had been dominated by cattle ranchers, and in her view "they were the salt of the earth." But Mingus and Thurber were populated by wage earners, a sort of subhuman species. Later, after national prohibition took over, many of the residents of foreign extraction called on their knowledge of wine making and brewing to bootleg. That put the capstone on Mother's hatred of the district. She well knew that when she was away from home and had to tell strangers where she lived, the look in their eyes would say, "Ah, ha, the wife of a bootlegger." However, Mingus did have two things in its favor: there was a Baptist church, which she never joined but always considered hers; and there was "Nigger Bill," William Wilhelm, the only black ever permitted to live in Mingus (no other black so much as dared to spend the night there). Bill was the janitor at the depot and soon became a close family friend.

Dad liked the town and the people. To him the rugged hills of the West Cross Timbers, covered with scrub oak and cedar, were nature's gift. He never tired of driving through them.

Shortly after settling in Mingus, Dad formed a partnership with Jeff Wright, and the two opened the Spratt & Wright Drug Store. Before he had been in town a year, he purchased the three-room house we had been renting and one-fourth of the city block on which it stood.

Mingus had no running water, so he had a cistern dug, lined with brick, and gutters put up to run rainwater into the cistern. We always drew water from the cistern by a rope and bucket. When mosquitoes found the cistern to be an ideal breeding place and began to show up in the house, Dad poured a cupful of coal oil into it to kill the wiggletails. For weeks, when drawing water, everyone had to be sure that the bucket sank to the very bottom of the cistern and was pulled up very quickly in an effort to get as little of the coal oil as possible. Dad had the front yard fenced with cypress palings and a wooden arch placed over the front gate. Painted white, its black boxcar lettering read "Dr. J. T. Spratt."

Here I grew up, living within a hundred yards of the main line of a transcontinental railroad. At that time, there was no better place for a boy to watch the world change before his very eyes.

2. Two Different Towns

THURBER AND Mingus were distinctly different towns. There was a fundamental reason for this: Thurber was owned in its entirety by the Texas & Pacific Coal Company, whereas Mingus was a railroad town with small proprietors. The major corporate entity in the latter was the Texas & Pacific Railway, whose local properties included a depot, switch tracks, coal chutes, water tank, and carshops. No one lived in Thurber other than company employees, members of the clergy, and schoolteachers. Even the doctors were company employees. Before my time, every employee of the company was required to live in Thurber, but a United Mine Workers local had changed this, and many miners, mine engineers, and other employees made their homes in Mingus or adjacent rural areas. Thurber was populated by a conglomerate of at least twenty different nationalities. In Mingus three or four Assyrian, a half dozen Italian, and some twelve Mexican families, plus one black, composed the non–Anglo Saxon segment. Although the two communities were related, they remained two different worlds.

Thurber was a company town, pure and simple. The Texas & Pacific Coal Company owned every square foot of land, every building, including churches, schools, and those used by fraternal orders, and every fixed piece of property. The company made all the decisions relative to land use, numbers and types of businesses, and even the size and location of the cemetery. Before Dad arrived, the company had belted Thurber with a barbed wire fence and placed armed guards at points of egress and ingress, with orders to keep out everyone who did not have the company blessing. This was in response to the Knights of Labor,* a union that had tried to organize the town. The

---

*The Knights of Labor, a national union of industrial workers, was organized in 1869 and by 1883 had grown to 700,000 members. Five district as-

Knights had appeared when the first coal was mined at Coalville, some eight miles northeast of Thurber, and the company (and its predecessor) had found their activities obnoxious. The fence not only blocked the troublesome Knights and other union organizers, but it also kept out hawkers, walkers and other peddlers, merchants, and even doctors.

In spite of company precautions, the United Mine Workers in 1903 organized the labor force at Thurber and saw that both the fence and the guards disappeared.* Outside merchants and doctors could freely advertise their wares or services in Thurber by the time my father settled in Mingus. Although the company employed its own doctors, Dad developed a larger practice in Thurber, which was in Erath County, than in Mingus, in Palo Pinto County.

In contrast to Thurber, Mingus was dominated by individual proprietorships. In the beginning, the only corporate property was the T&P Railroad, but in about 1910 the First State Bank obtained a corporate charter and opened its doors. The Loflin Mercantile Company, the lumberyard, and the Mingus Mercantile Company may have been corporate holdings, but I never knew for sure. The T&P also owned a two-story frame structure that housed the Van Noy Lunch Room on the first floor and hotel rooms on the second, but it burned before 1910 and was never rebuilt.

All who lived in Mingus could rent or buy a residence with as much land as they wished or could afford. Likewise, anyone could open a business. As a result, several groceries, two or three hardwares, three or four dry goods stores, and some six or eight saloons flourished at one time or another. There also were blacksmith, tin, and wood shops, several cafes and lunch counters, a watchmaker at times, plus temporary bakeshops and weekly newspapers such as the *Mingus Herald*. Spratt & Weber ran a drugstore and for a while had a competitor. When the neighboring Ranger oil boom occurred in 1917, a jackleg lawyer called Mingus home for a year or two. There was always one doctor, but now and then a second hung around for short periods. No facilities existed for regular entertainment until

---

semblies were active in Texas, with locals in Gordon and other mining centers. Unsuccessful strikes in 1886 weakened its western strength and it went into decline (Webb, *Handbook of Texas*, II, 2–3; Harold U. Faulkner, *American Economic History*, pp. 453–455).—Ed.

*The UMW, formed in 1890, had 43,000 members by the end of the decade. It developed strong locals in Texas, especially at Strawn and Lyra, a few miles from Thurber, and successfully unionized Thurber in 1903 (Allen, *Chapters*, p. 96; Faulkner, *American Economic History*, p. 457).—Ed.

after 1910. Several local men opened a small brewery, but their product failed to crack the beer market.

Early buildings in Mingus and Thurber were primarily of frame construction. Mingus boasted one brick residence in 1904, but its first brick business was not built until six years later, when a two-story structure was erected to house a bank. Attached was a one-story ell, which was rented out. When Bearden & Cox installed the first telephone system, they rented a room on the second floor for the exchange, and there they remained through the years, selling their business eventually to the Bradleys, who operated it as an independent system. Between 1910 and 1917, at least three brick stores, and about the same number of sheet iron buildings, appeared in Mingus.

Even though the T&P ran a brick plant at Thurber, the first major brick construction there was the tall smokestack for the boilers that drove the power and ice plants. By 1917 the company had erected a block of brick buildings to house the drugstore, post office, meat market, and company offices. A brick bandstand replaced the wooden one. The company also built tiers of brick homes for foremen and engineers. They were small and faced each other along one city block. These homes cost little more than the labor required to erect them, because the bricks were rejects from the company plant. After the T&P opened the Ranger oil field, it constructed a group of brick veneer homes on what was called New York Hill to accommodate the professional personnel brought in to supervise the company's large oil operations. The brick plant added more kilns and expanded production. Everything else in town was frame construction. This included homes of top management, clubs, churches, saloon, dance pavilion, hotel, school buildings, and residences for company workers.

As it owned all the residences, the company determined the shape, size, and location of each in Thurber. Houses contained three to five rooms, and costs per unit ranged from about $250.00. They were numbered, not by street and block, but in sequence as they were built. But knowing the house number did not ensure easy location; one must also be familiar with the various groupings. The houses were strewn about in an irregular manner and on small plots of ground. Since the Thurber grocery was company owned, lots were kept small to restrict family gardening. Occasionally, residents erected small pens for horses, but hogs roamed everywhere on the loose. Families of Latin extraction regularly grew chile peppers, which they threaded on strings and hung outside to dry. Morning glory vines climbed trellises to shade west doors and windows against the hot summer sun.

Beer drinkers sat and chatted under small, vine-covered arbors on

Sundays. Italians often played a ball game called "bochi,"* keeping near the arbor and its keg of beer. The game resembled horseshoe pitching, except that it was played with balls. A ball even served in lieu of the peg, or stake. A group might start playing bochi along the road and continue the game until they arrived at some designated shady nook in a pasture. There they would spend a greater part of the day drinking beer. Such treks generally were accompanied by a hack loaded with one or more kegs of beer, the number of kegs determined by the size of the party.

The residents of Thurber enjoyed certain conveniences. Most of the families drew water from an outside faucet, which served one or two houses. All homes had electricity, with single bulb drops in the center of each room. Coal provided fuel for both heating and cooking. In many yards, near the kitchen door, stood a beehive oven of stone, which Italian women used to bake huge (three-to-five-pound) loaves of native breads. These diamond-shaped loaves were porous and had beautiful brown crusts almost an inch thick. They were tasty beyond words.

In contrast to Thurber, Mingus was as orderly as a checkerboard. Streets and alleys ran north–south and east–west. An unoccupied lot in the center of town was designated "courthouse block" and was never offered for sale. Here, it was hoped, would sit the courthouse for an anticipated new county. Erath County was dry and so was Palo Pinto County, with the exception of Mingus precinct. The company saloon, the Snake, was located in the Mingus precinct, just north of the Erath County line. Many thought that efforts by prohibitionists to deny the coal miners their malt and alcoholic beverages would lead to an election to carve a new county from parts of Palo Pinto, Erath, and Eastland counties. Mingus, lying in the geographical center, would be the natural site for the county seat. The streets in Mingus had names, but the residents rarely used them. Families bought, rented, or poached land according to their ability or degree of honesty. Some acquired only an eighth of a block, but most settled on a quarter or half block.

Father started out with four lots in the southeast quarter of a block and subsequently acquired the entire block. This gave him room for a residence, office, separate barns for horses and cows, a chicken house and yard, a wash shed, pigsty, horse and cow lots, and a vegetable garden with two or three fruit trees and a few blackberry vines.

---

*Hardman, *Fire*, p. 130, and Gentry, "Thurber," p. 194, describe the game played with a boccie (bochi) ball.—Ed.

Adjoining the house was a fair-sized lawn, which served as a croquet court. A few families owned more land than we did, but most of them had one to three lots of fifty-foot widths.

As Mingus had no underground water mains, families relied on rainwater from dug cisterns or galvanized metal tanks, which rested on platforms under the eaves of houses. In addition, everybody kept large pickle or vinegar barrels near the fence to be filled regularly by Old Man Roark, who drove a water wagon pulled by a span of mules. Rainfall was unpredictable and no one dared to rely on cisterns or tanks exclusively. We used Roark water for family laundry, bathing, stock water, and hog killing. Roark pumped the water from a small pond in a creek bed outside of town, transported it in an oversized wooden barrel lying horizontally on a wagon frame, and filled barrels with a hose. He charged ten to fifteen cents per barrel, which ran the cost per thousand gallons to $3.00 to $4.50, a bit high. This system lasted until the 1930s, when the Works Progress Administration provided funds for Mingus to install water mains and pump water from Thurber Lake.

The streets of Thurber and Mingus were dirt thoroughfares, nothing more, and narrow. In the long dry spells, common to the West Cross Timbers region, wagon traffic ground the streets into dust six inches deep, sometimes deeper. Rain made them into quagmires. I remember seeing a middle-aged woman sloshing across a muddy street in Thurber and thinking, "Boy, she's either wearing boots or a pair of very high-topped galoshes." I was wrong. The woman was barefoot and the mud reached three or four inches above her ankles. Ruts became so deep that it was virtually impossible to pull a buggy or wagon out of them when meeting another vehicle. Sidewalks were mere trails along fences, changing to plank walks in front of business houses.

Outside town, dirt roads twisted through the countryside, trying desperately to pass the front gate of every farm. Narrow bridges spanned branches and creeks. If a driver came to a bridge occupied by a vehicle, he had to pull over and wait until it was clear. The approaches were short, steep dirt-fills, often rising at angles approaching thirty degrees. Floodwaters frequently washed out the approaches and halted traffic until they could be replaced. Buggies and wagons had no trouble navigating these dirt approaches, but they were grave menaces to early automobiles. With motors of less than thirty-five horsepower, autos could stall on these abrupt inclines with near-fatal results. Because the automobiles had no self-starters and unpredictable manual brakes, the driver had to let the car roll back to level ground. In the process, drivers often lost control and the car overturned, pinning the passengers beneath. Many were crippled and some were killed in such accidents. Fortunately, the light weight of the cars saved most from death.

The first improved streets in Thurber and Mingus were covered with cinders. This substitute for macadam was plentiful and cheap. In the yards and along the main line men knocked cinders from locomotive fireboxes and daily shoveled them from between the rails to the side of the tracks. The practice was costly and time consuming. Old Poncho, the tallest Mexican-American section hand I ever saw, was permanently assigned to clearing the main tracks in Mingus. Our house was on a level with these tracks, but at times cinders lined a half mile of embankment to a height of three feet, making it impossible for us to see a building across the tracks. Periodically, the railroad crews loaded these cinder piles into gondolas and hauled them away. The cycle then started again.

The T&P soon found a local use for the old cinders. Crews began scooping the cinders into wagons and spreading the gritty material on the road to Thurber. Traffic pulverized the cinders in a short time, and the mud and dust problem quickly faded. Dad had several loads spread on the streets in front of and to the side of our house. Mingus businessmen carpeted two or three blocks in the downtown section. Thurber also dumped cinders on its streets and even along sidewalks. Cinders provided the major improvement in road building around Mingus and Thurber until the eve of World War I.

By 1914 the residents of Mingus were enjoying electricity in their homes. The power source, individually owned and operated, was located in Gordon and consisted of a small dynamo pulled by a ten-horsepower gasoline engine housed in a small galvanized iron shanty. From this point, lines ran three miles to Mingus. For years we only had electricity in the evening, from six o'clock until midnight, seven days a week. The exception was Wednesday morning, when the company provided power from eight until noon for ironing. If a housewife failed to have her ironing ready for Wednesday, she could either try it at night or wait a week. In each room of the house a light cord and socket hung from the center of the ceiling. The bulb might exceed twenty-five watts, but many of them were no more than fifteen. Lighting was poor, but it was much better than the illumination from a kerosene lamp. The use of an electric appliance was out of the question. Lights not only were installed in homes, but also were placed in churches, lodge halls, and the depot. The only businesses in Mingus that sported electric lights were the pool hall, drugstore, and saloons.

Previously, our lighting had come from coal oil lamps or lanterns.

They lighted not only the homes, but also the depot, evening church services, and lodge halls. Summer evangelists used gasoline torches because they held revival meetings outside under brush arbors— never inside the church. Gusts of wind created problems with coal oil lamps, frequently extinguishing the gospel light just as a soul stood at the brink of salvation. Gasoline torches, with tongues of flame radiating like spokes of a wheel from a central burner, danced and pranced in the strongest gales, but never went out. At home, my brother, Harry,* and I studied by small lamps that held a half cup of kerosene and provided a half candlepower of light. These lamps sat on our desk, a homemade table about five feet long, constructed from an old box.

Thurber was one of the first towns in Texas to be fully electrified. Its plant furnished ten thousand inhabitants with power twenty-four hours a day. Its opera house was the first building in Texas used for public entertainment to be equipped with ceiling fans. The power plant sent electricity not only to homes, offices, businesses, lodges, churches, bandstand, and dance pavilion, but also to its industrial complex. For example, it fed power to the electric donkey, which pulled cars full of clay to the brick plant from a hill more than a mile away. When electric motors replaced burros in the mines, each mine generated its own power. Thurber was not only far in advance of Mingus in the use of electricity, but it was also well ahead of most Texas towns at that time.

In some respects, the company ice plant was more important to Thurber than its light plant. Here, machinery produced ice for the town and chilled the largest storage vault in the state. Hundreds of beeves and other carcasses could be kept frozen there. This vault was really an adjunct of the company meat market. With people of more different national origins residing in Thurber than anywhere else in Texas, except possibly Galveston, the market prepared meats according to dozens of recipes. Actually, the Thurber market processed a greater variety of meats than came from the combined output of the Swift and Armour packing plants in Fort Worth. As part of the company's paternalistic philosophy, managers perhaps felt that meats prepared to national tastes were a good antidote to homesickness for the "Old Country." Herds of cattle from fifty to seventy-five miles away were driven to Thurber for sale to the meat market.

For years Mingus obtained its ice by rail from Weatherford or Fort Worth. A yard crew pushed huge blocks along a slide from a refrig-

---

*William Harry Spratt (July 11, 1904–September 23, 1970).—Ed.

erated car to an ice vault, which housed perishable merchandise. Novitt & Hoffman, who stored bananas there, made more money from the use of the icehouse than any other customer, including saloonkeepers who stored beer there. A certain amount of ice was peddled to Mingus residents. During the early decades, ice was cheap. It retailed at ten pounds for ten cents to one hundred pounds for forty cents. Family iceboxes varied in size, with large compartments holding blocks weighing up to one hundred pounds. Melting water from the ice dripped from a spout through a hole drilled in the floor or into a large pan shoved under the box. Housewives emptied these basins once a day. This ice water was very soft and excellent for cooking frijoles or for washing hair.

Thurber was never incorporated nor did it have governmental machinery. For law enforcement the T&P paid the salary of a deputy sheriff, who lived in town. The Thurber school district never issued a school bond nor levied a school tax. The T&P furnished the school building, hired teachers, collected the per scholastic payment from the state, and paid operational costs out of its own funds. Nor was there ever a road bond issue. No resident of Thurber rendered tangible property for taxation, so no one was eligible to vote on either bonds or tax rates. Because of the large Catholic population in Thurber, the company permitted the church to run a parochial school on its property and likely gave the school some financial support.

Mingus presented a different picture. Every property owner paid taxes. These taxpayers voted to establish the Mingus Independent School District and sanctioned a bond issue for the construction of a two-story brick building. In addition, they approved tax rates for retiring the bonds, building maintenance, and teacher salaries. Thurber may have had better-qualified teachers than Mingus. I did not have a teacher with more than summer normal training until I reached the seventh grade, when the school board hired several who had two years of college training. I was a high school freshman in Strawn when I encountered a teacher with a college degree. I am not sure that the quality of the two schools made a great difference. The dropout rate was high at both places, especially among the boys, who took jobs in the mines at sixteen. Girls quit school to marry. Only two or three of my classmates finished both high school and college.

There was no need for a bank in Thurber. The company paid its employees in cash twice each month, and anyone who ran short between paydays could draw company scrip. The cash value of the scrip was deducted from the next pay envelope. Scrip did away with the expense of keeping charge account records and largely eliminated the need for bank credit. For many years, the company refused to honor scrip spent anywhere except at a company store. Again, the union stepped in and worked out an agreement whereby the company would honor scrip wherever it might be spent. This did not hurt the trade at the company stores, because at least 90 percent of the scrip issued was still spent there. For those Thurberites who did need a bank, the Mingus State Bank offered its services. It was a good-sized bank, especially for our little community.

Contrary to company practice in Thurber, Mingus merchants extended credit. Several firms sent hacks to Thurber every day, delivering orders taken on the previous day and at the same time taking orders for the next day. Others sent a man to spend the day seeking orders. Joe Abraham, an Assyrian groceryman in Mingus, once told me that if he failed to collect at least ten thousand dollars from his Thurber customers on the first and fifteenth of each month, he thought business for the fortnight was slow. That represented the sale of a sizable quantity of merchandise at a time when salt pork retailed at five or ten cents a pound, round steak at twenty-five cents a pound, Arbuckle Coffee at fifteen to twenty-five cents a pound, and coal oil at ten cents a gallon.

Joe's was a typical small-town grocery store. There were no small-lot deliveries. Flour, cornmeal, sugar, and other staples came in carload lots by rail, as did bran and corn chops. Barrels of pickles, coffee, cheese, dried beans and fruits, crackers, salt and canned goods came in LCL (less-than-carload lots). Of necessity, more than half of Joe's working capital was tied up in a slow-moving inventory. The rate of turnover did not exceed three times a year.

Men the world over who do dusty work usually consume large quantities of wines or malt liquors. Coal miners in Thurber and Mingus were no exception. The Snake, just across the line in Palo Pinto County and Thurber's only saloon, boasted the longest horse-shoe bar in the world, and each afternoon it quickly filled when the men returned from the mines. As many as twenty-five bartenders were on duty during this rush period. Even at that, those not in the front line had to wait fifteen to twenty minutes before being served. They all wanted tap beer, and pint schooners were the smallest amounts served. Filling pint and quart schooners, or quart or gallon pails, was time consuming. Prices, depending on the quantity, ranged from five to twenty-five cents. Those ordering schooners did their drinking inside the saloon, while the men with gallon pails either went on home or sought a bench outside the saloon to sit, sip, and visit with friends. Beer drinking did little to rid men of "black lung," but it quickly washed coal dust from dry mouths and throats. The Snake Saloon sold on the average seven carloads of beer each week.

The saloons in Mingus dispensed only a carload of beer each week, and 90 percent of the sales were to railroad employees. There was no demand for wine, for most of the miners were from wine-drinking regions and made their own brew. Whiskey consumption also was low, with the combined saloons in town selling less than a carload lot each week. Special orders for liquor was a common practice. Each Saturday the westbound passenger train dropped off an express car of beer at Mingus. This car had been ordered by individuals or groups for Sunday drinking.

Old Sam Graves was the owner, operator, bartender, and janitor of one of the Mingus saloons. He had little time to clean his place during the week, so he reserved this chore for Sunday mornings. The Methodist and Baptist churches in Mingus were just over two blocks apart, and Sam lived halfway between them. Services at both churches were usually closing about the time Sam reached home from his saloon cleaning. As he reached his gate one Sunday morning, the congregations were singing their closing hymns. To his left, the Methodists were singing, "Will there be any stars, any stars in my crown?" From his right came the Baptist refrain, "No not one, no not one."

Open saloons came to a sudden end with the adoption of the Eighteenth Amendment to the Constitution in 1919. The Snake closed, never to reopen. National prohibition caused enormous property destruction, as millions of dollars' worth of machinery and equipment went to scrapyards. Saloon furnishings sold for as little as ten cents on the dollar. Dad bought a large whiskey case from the White Maple Bar in Fort Worth, paying $25.00 for what had cost $250.00. He placed the case in his office to serve as a bookshelf.

During the Christmas and New Year seasons, on making his rounds, Dad would often find the trunk of his coupe filled with bottles of home brew, placed there while he was inside visiting patients. When he got home he put the bottles in gunnysacks, drove out to Palo Pinto Creek, and dumped the lot from a high cliff. "Nobody but a fool would drink that stuff," he said.

Prior to Prohibition, virtually all incoming freight billed to Thurber had originated in the East. With Prohibition, however, carloads of freight began to arrive from the West. The cargoes were grapes, either fresh or dried, from California vineyards. Thurber residents who came from wine-producing countries saw nothing sinful or illegal in making and drinking homemade wine. For a time, those not familiar with wine making were instructed in the art by labels on the bricks of dried grapes from California growers. They circumvented the law against giving instructions on how to produce alcoholic beverages by warning buyers not to put the package of grapes in so many gallons of water, not to add so many pounds of sugar, and not to keep the mixture at a specific temperature for so many days. If a person did so, he produced fermentation, which was illegal.

Those who did not care for wine began brewing a concoction known as "chock beer." But neither of these beverages had the kick to satisfy the hard drinkers. As a result, clandestine stills began turning out corn whiskey or "white mule." News gradually spread through the alcohol desert of North Texas that those with parched throats could get relief in the Thurber-Mingus district.

3. The Lifeline

FOR MORE than three decades, the coal-burning locomotives of the Texas & Pacific Railway served as the Thurber-Mingus lifeline to the outside world. Through the years, these rail gluttons consumed millions of tons of coal. In fact, they burned more than 90 percent of the coal mined at Thurber. Some one hundred cars of coal left the Mingus freight yards each day to be distributed at coaling points along the T&P for its locomotives. Eventually, changing technology produced a cheaper and more efficient fuel in petroleum, and these insatiable steam engines became obsolete. Their fate signaled the end of an era for both Thurber and Mingus. Yet during their day, the coal burners and their crews furnished the substance for a thousand sagas.

The Texas & Pacific Railway in 1904 was a tenuous network. In his mad race in the early 1880s to put the T&P into El Paso before the Southern Pacific got there, Jay Gould built a flimsy railroad. Along a dirt roadbed with no ballast, crews spaced thousands of crossties, binding them together with light steel rails that weighed less than eighty pounds to the yard. The heads of the rails were so narrow that a tightwire walker would have had difficulty staying on one. In Mingus on Sunday afternoons, a favorite pastime for a boy and his girl was trying to balance on these rails. This was thrilling because it provided an extra opportunity for holding hands in public in broad daylight.

Locomotives, both freight and passenger, were small and light. Coaches and freight cars were built of wood. Whenever bad wrecks occurred, a pile of kindling might be strewn for several hundred yards along the track. Cargoes in excess of thirty tons were heavy loads, and boxcars generally had a top load limit of forty tons. Few freight trains contained twenty cars, and for years their maximum road speed was fixed at twelve miles per hour. Passenger trains running between Fort Worth and El Paso made the six-hundred-mile run in twenty-four to thirty hours. It was the topic of conversation among T&P employees for weeks, when it was announced that the railroad's crack passenger train, the Sunshine Special, had been scheduled to make the run in eighteen hours.

Maintenance costs of the road were high. Section crews were housed along the line at ten-mile intervals, sometimes closer. For example, the distance from Gordon through Mingus to Strawn was eight miles, but section crews were stationed in each town. Out in the semidesert West, one passed an isolated section camp about every ten miles. A foreman and eight or ten men made up an average gang. Six, sometimes seven, days of the week, they labored as "steel-driving men." The days were long and bad weather added extra burdens. Washouts and train wrecks demanded the concentration of several section crews for work around the clock until the road was back in service.

As coal-burning locomotives consumed great quantities of fuel and water, the T&P built regular points of replenishment. Coal chutes were widely separated. For example, there was a chute at Mingus, but the next one was at Fort Worth, seventy miles to the east. Until 1916 the railroad hauled locomotive water to Mingus in wooden tank cars, but by 1920 the T&P created a lake by throwing a dam across a creek on the outskirts of town to impound water for its engines. There were two reasons for this. First, locomotives regularly took on coal in Mingus, and it was logical to fill their water tanks there at the same time. Second, as larger engines came into use, they consumed more water. There must have been twice as many water stops along the line as there were coaling stations.

On family trips to Pecos as a kid, I remember seeing these pump stations and water tanks. They were located in the middle of nowhere, and pumpers, leaning against a shanty, always waved at passengers on the train. I thought they must be the loneliest people in the world. A man had to be stationed at each stop because there was no electricity available to trigger the pump when water reached a low level in the tank. Where no underground water was discovered by drilling, the railroad refilled the water tanks by special cars, and in some places, dug large earthen reservoirs to impound water for long periods of dry weather.

Coal chutes consisted of several contiguous bins, each with a trapdoor for releasing its contents into locomotive tenders. Cars loaded with coal were parked beside the bins, and ten or more men labored there twenty-four hours a day, breaking up huge chunks of coal into pieces suitable for fireboxes and shoveling it into the bins. The bins held different tonnages because when the fireman pulled the trap there was no way to stop the flow of coal until the bin was empty. In 1916 the T&P tore down the old chutes and installed a towerlike automatic chute, which could be operated by one man. The new facility had a basement below track level with machinery there to pulverize coal. A switch engine pushed loaded gondolas to the chute and the sides of the cars dropped, spilling coal down on an iron grate with six-inch squares. The larger pieces that did not pass into a basement were broken up by hand. In the basement, a pulverizer worked over the coal, and an endless belt hoisted it fifty feet to the bins. Coal flowed to a locomotive tender through a trough that swung on hinges. The fireman pulled the trough downward to the tender and opened the trapdoor by a tug on a cord. When the cord was released, the door shut. This gave the fireman complete control of the flow of coal.

In Mingus the coal chutes sat on the edge of a slope leading down to Palo Pinto Creek. It was an awkward location. There was always a possibility that the coal cars, usually five, might break loose, loaded or empty, and head down the slope. Such a mishap would have meant a certain wreck, with cars piled all over the tracks of the main line. By 1910 a new set of chutes was built east of Mingus, with a side track to carry coal gondolas from the main line in case of an emergency. But this operation did not last long. The T&P converted its locomotives to oil and replaced the coal chutes with a large tank that would hold several thousand barrels of oil. When diesel locomotives appeared, the oil tank was dismantled and sold for scrap and the concrete water towers, built with an automatic trigger to refill from an electric pump, were abandoned. Standing gray and empty, these towers became true ghosts along the tracks.

The last of the T&P coal burners, traveling on 110-pound rails, were giants. Larger engines demanded larger tenders, and on an average run these monsters consumed tons of coal and water by the thousands of gallons. Tenders carried from six to thirty tons. After conversion to oil, the smallest engine I knew of had a tender capacity of 1,400 gallons of oil and 3,600 gallons of water.

Engine wheels varied from small 0-6-0s to the giant 2-10-4s and 4-8-2s. The middle number indicated the number of major driving wheels. Weights of engines, minus the tenders, ranged from 95,000 pounds to 307,000; weights of engines and tenders increased over time from 220,000 to 739,000 pounds. Traction power applied to the rails by the wheels increased from 19,400 pounds, with 13,300 coming from smaller booster wheels. Practically all the giant engines were equipped with boosters. The boosters gave added power in starting long and heavy trains and provided an extra push in moving heavy trains up grades. Small locomotives never had boosters.

As larger, more powerful, and speedier locomotives joined the fleet, a revolution in railroading occurred. Freight trains lengthened from thirty to over one hundred cars, and passenger trains grew from five coaches to sixteen or more. Longer passing sidings were added, and an automatic block system was installed for greater safety of life and rolling stock. Around the railroad shops, there was considerable speculation as to how long it would be before the T&P had to double-track its road. This was never needed because railroads found ways to operate a single track at 70 percent of the capacity of a double track.

Whether pulling work trains, loaded gondolas, or freight and passenger trains, locomotives poured tons of coal smoke and dust into the air. The two work trains that left Thurber each morning for the mines were segregated by color and national origin, but when they returned in the late afternoon every coach was completely integrated. No one could tell Jew from Gentile, Italian from Czech, or black from white. They had labored in coal dust throughout the day, and it made black men of them all. After several years, the union persuaded the company to provide washhouses at the mines. From then on, the coaches bearing the workers to and from work remained segregated.

Everything that moved seemed to pour coal particles into the air. On each of the six workdays of the week, five coal-burning switch engines huffed and puffed around the clock, shuttling over one hundred cars from the mines near Thurber to Mingus and taking empties back to the mines. In the yards, they switched cars to and fro, making up trains for distribution. Coal-burning engines also powered all the machinery in Thurber, particularly the ice and power plants. Coal heated the kilns at the brick plant. In Mingus, scores of coal-burning locomotives daily passed through town hauling eight or ten passenger trains east and west. Each stopped and spent five minutes to an hour spreading smoke over the countryside. The coal chutes at Mingus added a goodly amount of dust to the air, as crews broke big chunks into small pieces suitable for locomotive fireboxes. Clouds of black dust rose when coal from the chutes crashed into a locomotive tender.

No one dared hang out laundry until the clothesline had been wiped clean with a damp cloth. Not to do so meant a heavy black line at every point the freshly laundered piece touched the wire. It was not unusual to redo an entire wash because a standing locomotive heaved mighty puffs of soot into the air when it lurched to put a heavy train in motion. The settling soot quickly turned snow-white sheets into black shrouds.

Traveling in a wooden passenger coach was an interesting experience. Small pot-bellied coal heaters stood at the ends of each car to furnish heat in cold weather. In hot weather, passengers raised the car windows to relieve the discomfort and enjoy the draft created by the moving train. Along with the draft came cinders from the engine's smokestack. If the train ran through a whirlwind or a sandstorm, these cinders collected on the begrimed windowsills, turning white shirts coal black in just a few moments.

The Spratts always traveled like Hetty Green;* that is, we rode in a chair car to and from Pecos and El Paso. And like Hetty, we carried our fried chicken and biscuits in shoe boxes. Cinders got into the food, but you could easily wash them down with a bottle of strawberry soda pop. The coaches provided water coolers, one to a car, with ice being added at every division stop. There also were toilets— just a seat over a straight pipe, eight or ten inches in diameter, which extended straight down about three feet toward the tracks.

During the day, the trains made meal stops in Mingus. A westbound always stopped "twenty minutes for dinner." There were up to three family-operated lunchrooms near the depot to feed travelers. Meals began at twenty-five cents. "Hot Tamale" Bates met both east- and westbound locals, offering tamales for fifteen cents a dozen, or two dozen for a quarter. Sam Heath and other schoolboys frequently paraded along the side of the train, peddling fried chicken and biscuits for ten cents, three for a quarter. The eastbound train arrived at three in the afternoon with only a five- or ten-minute stop, but Bates and the chicken-and-bread boys were usually there.

Every train carried a news butcher, who made regular trips through the cars with a small assortment of food and reading material. The butch on No. 3, westbound, usually climbed down from the train at Mingus and circulated around the depot with an armful of the *Fort Worth Star Telegram* and two or three copies of the *Dallas Morning News* while the passengers and train crew ate lunch. Few persons in Mingus subscribed to daily papers, nor did the drugstore have a paper agency. Thus the butch provided a chance to keep up with happenings in the outside world. The butch also sold books. Neither Mingus or Thurber had public or school libraries, nor were books sold in either

---

*Henrietta (Hetty) Robinson Green inherited $10 million in 1865 and developed a financial empire worth $100 million by the time of her death in 1916. Her son, Edward H. G. Green, built the Texas Midland Railroad. A person with simple tastes, Hetty was regarded as an eccentric by many ("Henrietta [Hetty] Robinson Green," *National Cyclopaedia of American Biography*, XV, 128).—Ed.

town. From the news butch, one could buy a variety of paperbacks. Popular selections included *The Story of Cole Younger*, tales about the James Brothers, Capt. William F. Drannan's pack of lies in *Thirty-one Years on the Plains*, classics such as *Ten Nights in a Bar-room* and *Great Train Robberies*, and many others. News butchers also peddled little glass railroad lanterns, locomotives, pistols filled with candies, as well as apples, soda pop, oranges, and ham sandwiches. Although the sandwiches were flat and dry, I thought they were the most delectable goodies ever offered to man.

At dusk one summer evening, my father was called to a home located near the coal chutes. The family there had heard a baby crying just after eastbound No. 4 had stopped for coal. When the cries continued, always from the same direction, they decided to investigate and found a babe in the creek bed below the railroad trestle. Evidence revealed that the child had been dropped from the train through the toilet pipe. Father had the depot agent wire Fort Worth and inquire if passengers on No. 4 had reported a baby missing. Railroad officials investigated and reported that indeed a child had been deliberately dropped from the train, and who dropped it.

Early next morning Dad and Bob Loflin, the deputy sheriff, caught the train with the baby and headed for Fort Worth. They were met at the station by a prominent local citizen whose daughter had chosen to ditch an infant she did not want. The grandfather gave the doctor and the deputy one hundred dollars each, and they caught the No. 3 back to Mingus. That ended the story, except that the family who found the baby under the T&P bridge, not knowing its name, had briefly called him "T. P. Mingus."

Passenger trains were segregated in two ways in the early days. There was the Jim Crow coach, or half coach, on short trains with "Colored" signs plainly displayed. Whites would be evicted from such areas, as a black would be removed from white coaches. Then there was the smoking car. Men who wished to smoke, and only men smoked in those days, were required to go to this area to enjoy a cigar, pipe, or cigarette. Here also traveled the drummer, with his display case or cases. Lighted cigars, derby hats, and blue serge suits were common trademarks. Riding together in the smokers, they could puff away, exchange market information, and try to top each other with yarns, clean or smutty.

Word once spread in Mingus that ex-President Teddy Roosevelt would pass through town on a certain day by special train going to El Paso to meet the president of Mexico in Juárez. The train was due to arrive at noon; that meant that the ex-president would stop twenty minutes for dinner. My father reminded me that I had seen Roosevelt when I was about the age of three.* Word had come that the president would visit Fort Worth, so Dad took the family to see him. In probably my earliest recollection, I faintly remember a mass of people jostling each other on a sidewalk. I was perched on my father's shoulder and my mother was at his side with my baby brother in her arms. Suddenly a hansom cab drawn by shiny black horses came into view. In the cab stood a man with a big mustache, a broad grin, and large teeth. He was dressed in a cutaway coat and waved a top hat at the crowd. There the picture fades.

I was anxious to see Teddy again. On the appointed day, school was let out early, and all the kids marched down to the depot. Quite a crowd had gathered there. Soon someone yelled, "There she comes!" The engineer was playing his whistle to keep the track clear. It was a three-car special—but it did not stop. As the last car passed, Teddy popped out onto the observation platform and gave several hundred Democrats and two Republicans a big wave, plus a grin that must have bared all but four of his big teeth.† This was the first time that Mingus learned that trains could and did carry dining cars. It was a shocking discovery.

Mingus, however, got a consolation prize. William Jennings Bryan stopped off "twenty minutes" at a lunch counter while he was secretary of state.** The meal was served family style and included a large plate of radishes, most of which were not eaten. Bryan was very fond of radishes, and on getting up from the table he picked up the radish dish, poured its contents into his coat pocket to munch on later, and boarded the train.

For years, the T&P advertised the Cannon Ball as its crack passenger train between St. Louis and El Paso. From what we saw in Mingus, it must have been the slowest-moving cannonball in history. The distance was about thirteen hundred miles, and the train's

*Pres. Theodore Roosevelt visited Fort Worth on April 8, 1905, to go wolf hunting with rancher-oilmen Burk Burnett and Tom Waggoner (Oliver Knight, *Fort Worth: Outpost on the Trinity*, pp. 168–169). Reporters said twenty thousand people were at the T&P station in Fort Worth to see the president.—Ed.

† Roosevelt passed through Mingus en route to El Paso on the T&P in mid-March of 1911 (Knight, *Fort Worth*, p. 169; *New York Times*, March 16, 1911).—Ed.

**William Jennings Bryan, the ever-popular Democrat, was secretary of state from 1913 to 1915. He passed through Mingus on February 20, 1912 (Mary A. Sarber, El Paso Public Library, to Harwood P. Hinton, December 4, 1984, editor's files).—Ed.

running time was forty-eight hours. If cannonballs fired by the Confederate batteries on the cliffs at Vicksburg had traveled no faster than the T&P's Cannon Ball, they would have rolled down the cliff to the river, and Grant would have taken the town without a lengthy siege. The train was replaced by the Sunshine Special, which had steel passenger coaches sporting steam heat and water toilets, powerful locomotives, and a dining car. It trimmed the running time between Fort Worth and El Paso by six hours, primarily by reducing station stops and cutting the train to one mail-baggage car, a diner, observation car, and pullman.

Every division point along the T&P had its own wrecker. The contraption in the Mingus yards was a wooden beam some thirty feet long, made of four-by-twelves bolted together and fastened to a huge swivel in the middle of a flatcar. It could be swung to either side of the car and elevated to an angle of forty-five degrees. The lifting power centered in a huge wooden block and tackle, threaded with two-inch manila hawsers, which hung from the free end of the beam. After a hawser was fastened to the overturned car or locomotive, the other end of the rope was tied to a switch engine, which slowly backed away in hopes that the beam and its block would bring the damaged car back onto the rails or would lift it to an upright position. But the lifting power of this wooden wrecker was unpredictable. A hawser would snap when the car or engine had been half-righted, or a lateral overstrain might upset the flatcar and its hoist. When locomotives became larger and steel replaced wood in cars, the old wreckers failed completely. They were replaced by wreckers that supported heavy steel cranes and utilized steel cables operated by donkey engines.

Sometimes, trains suffered delays because of a sudden change in climatic conditions. As a kid, I once sat on a T&P passenger train for nearly eight hours in the middle of nowhere west of Midland as a blazing sun bored through a brassy sky. A cloudburst had swept the land. There probably had not been enough rain at any one time in a hundred years to drown out a good-sized prairie dog town, but floodwaters now had created a lake stretching to the horizon. It engulfed the railroad up to a depth of five or six feet for a mile along the tracks. The water would have swamped the firebox if the locomotive had rushed into it.

The railroad hired every man and team in that locale, and they worked continuously, trying to open a drainage canal that would lower the lake. Men regularly waded back and forth to determine its depth. Finally, a foreman signaled that the water had dropped and ordered the train to proceed. We moved at a snail's pace behind a man who waded ahead to make sure that the engine would not be swamped and finally made it to the other side of the lake and moved on.

To me, big steam locomotives and big men were concomitants. Among the many engineers I knew as a teenager (and I had an obsession for trains), only one was a small man. A huge steam locomotive, either coal or oil burner, represented awesome majesty. Poised at the head of the train, freight or passenger, this giant iron monster emitted latent power in every jet of steam spewing from an injector as it forced water into the boiler, and the regular cadence of subdued puffs bounced gently from the smokestack. Every whistle on these iron horses had its own distinctive blast. The sounds ranged from high soprano to resonant low basso. When an engineer opened the throttle, the monster came alive, producing chuggings that exploded balls of black smoke skyward. With steam spewing from its exhaust valves, every person in sight and hearing recognized that a dragon was being roused into action.

The coal-burning locomotive not only tied Mingus to Thurber, but also placed it on a major highway of steel that vitally influenced the lives of its citizens. Mingus drew its lifeblood from the coal mines at Thurber, but at the same time, it experienced the benefits and liabilities of a railroad town. As a longtime resident, I derived a considerable education from studying the trains that gave dimension and color to our community.

4. Life in Thurber

THE WORKING families who lived in Thurber had few watches or clocks, for their daily lives were governed by whistles. At the company power plant, engineers scanned clocks with large dials and numbers and sounded the whistles at designated times. Residents soon learned the hours of the day and night when whistles were blown and the meaning of each blast. During a workday, a whistle awakened the sleeping town, warned it that trains were leaving for the mines, and told the men when to begin work, take off for lunch, end their lunchtime, and quit for the day. These same whistles kept the women in town informed of the day's schedule. Housewives knew almost to the minute how long it would take a switch engine to haul the coaches back to town loaded with hungry miners. These whistles, as resonant as steamboat blasts, also guided the movements of miner households in Mingus, two miles away.

In Mingus we heard other whistles. Passenger trains regularly announced their approach, varying little from schedule. Westbound No. 7 warned that midday was at hand. Eastbound No. 4 reminded us that school would let out within forty minutes. Westbound No. 5 advised that midnight was at hand. Eastbound No. 6 blasted away at 4:00 A.M. In addition, whistles from passing freights broke the silence at all hours of the day and night. When locomotive whistles in Mingus began erratic blasts, townspeople knew there was grave trouble, probably a home on fire. Cries of "Fire! Fire!" came from every direction, as men with buckets raced toward the smoke and went into action, splashing water on the burning walls. Every community member momentarily considered himself a hero in trying to save his neighbor's property, but in most cases, efforts fizzled completely.

In Thurber the workday began with the 4:00 A.M. whistle, which aroused sound sleepers and those who walked two or three miles to catch the train to the mines. At the 5:00 blast, breakfast was under way, and lunch pails, miners' caps and torches, work jackets, and a tobacco supply should all be in hand. The 6:00 whistle warned that the work train to the mines, called the Black Diamond, would soon leave. The 8:00 whistle started the shift, which stopped for lunch at the 12:00 whistle and went back to work at its 1:00 blast. Miners hurried to the cages to be lifted to the surface at the sound of the 5:00 whistle. There they clambered aboard Old Black Diamond (the work shuttle) for the ride to Thurber.

While men were at work in the mines, downtown Thurber was largely deserted. A few women might be seen on the streets going to or from the stores or market, but most of them remained at home. They had bread to bake, laundry to do, along with a half dozen other household chores. Preparation of the evening meal took a good part of the day. Driving about Thurber in the afternoon was an aromatic treat. Foods pleasing to twenty or more foreign tastes emitted distinctive aromas. A visitor to Thurber from any part of the world could easily have found some home where his favorite food was being prepared.

Other "Old Country" practices retained in Thurber, at least through the first generation, included home weaving. I treasured a scrap of linen from a piece woven by an Italian woman for her husband, John. The cloth was thick and the weave was tight. Three or four shirts made from such cloth would have lasted a lifetime.

Thurber women also spent considerable time preparing for festivities—national, religious, and social. Different groups celebrated "Old Country" holidays with gala folk dances, brightened by the wearing of native costumes. Weddings topped all celebrations for most families. Women spent weeks sewing wedding garments, which often were very elaborate, and labored long hours in the kitchen cooking enough food for an army. The wine supply extended well beyond the departure of the last guest. And the host family always had an orchestra on hand to play for the dancing to favorite tunes.

Everyone participated in the two annual holidays that were American in origin. The company set aside three days for picnics on July 4 and on Labor Day. Everybody in Thurber, plus hundreds of people from miles around, turned out for these affairs. On each occasion, there was a carnival, the Thurber band provided concerts, and the crowd danced in the pavilion.

Christmas climaxed the year for everyone. There may have been a few Moslems in Thurber, but I never knew one there or in Mingus. Nor were there many Jews in the two towns. The few who lived there invariably went to Fort Worth to celebrate Jewish festive or religious days. Whether Jewish, Moslem, Hindu, Chinese, or Christian, the townsfolk enjoyed the holiday season and participated in the parties that closed out the old Gregorian year and welcomed the new.

The Thurber wife, who was the center of all household activities, contributed greatly in keeping old country customs alive and vital. This may have been due, in part, to the fact that wives of foreign extraction had less contact with the English-speaking majority than did the men. I knew some women of foreign birth who, after sixty years of residence in this country, could not carry on the simplest conversation in English.

Coal mining at Thurber was fraught with occupational hazards. Every time a man went down a shaft to mine coal, he walked and worked where crippling accidents or sudden death could occur at any time. Over the years, his working area also made him a victim of the "black lung." Mining and moving coal created a fine dust that blackened face and hands, crept into every pore of the body, and ground deeply into the clothing. Coal mining in Thurber was particularly hard work. Most of the veins were thirty-six inches thick, and miners had to dig from a prone position. As a result they wallowed in beds of coal dust all day long and breathed dust caused by pick and shovel and loading operations.

Every mine had two shafts, which were located some distance apart. The larger shaft permitted two cages to operate side by side. The cages were raised and lowered by a cable that was wound around a large drum and attached to a donkey engine. When one cage went down, the other came up. Miners rode these cages to and from work levels morning and afternoon, but during the day the cages hauled carts of coal to the surface. Whether carrying men or coal, the engineer moved the cars up and down the shaft at the same speed—fast.

Over the second shaft sat a frame housing with a huge fan. The fan was at least twenty feet in diameter, with dozens of blades three or four feet in length and a foot wide, extending out in a horizontal position. The outer edges were curved so that the fan, spinning counterclockwise, sucked foul air from the mine and at the same time pushed a supply of fresh air down the shaft. The fan operated continuously. In case the elevator shaft became blocked, the air shaft became an emergency exit. In addition to circulating fresh air through the mines, these fans also sucked out poisonous or flammable gases.

There may have been fatalities in the Thurber mines from gas explosions or from inhaling poisonous gases, but I cannot recall hearing of such deaths. However, at times, men were killed or maimed when some careless act ignited a keg of blasting powder. These kegs were kept in the mines because the men embedded small charges of the powder in the veins and ignited them to blast the coal loose for easier mining.

The company used burros deep in the mines and aboveground to pull cars. The animals working underground lived there. They drew loaded coal cars along a small, narrow track to the cage, where they were lifted to the surface. The burros stabled aboveground hauled cars of slate and other impurities cleaned from the coal out to the dump. As they could not maneuver a heavy car up an incline of more than two or three degrees, the dumps were long and flat. Later, donkey engines pulled slate cars to the tops of the dumps, where they were automatically tipped, then allowed to roll back down the track for another load. These slate piles resembled huge, inverted ice cream cones. A quick glance at a dump easily revealed whether it dated from the burro days.

About 1910 the company replaced the burros with electric generators. Power lines were run down the shaft and along the drifts to drive electric cars to haul coal. Crews also strung lights through the long passageways excavated near the coal veins to permit men to walk upright. These supplemented the carbide lamps fastened to the miners' caps. Despite better light, men still had to mine coal from a prone position, at right angles to these passageways, and perform the backbreaking labor of shoveling the diggings into cars for removal to the surface. The daily output of a miner varied, but the average ranged from two to three tons. A man who dug five or more tons a day was a gem.

I have no idea what happened to the burros.* Perhaps they were sold, although the price per animal would have been no more than three dollars. Perhaps they were turned loose to roam. I do know that every boy in Mingus, except Harry and me, soon had a donkey. It was great fun to take off down the road while perched on the rump of a galloping burro. The two Spratt brothers pleaded for a donkey, but our pleas were ignored. Maybe Dad reasoned that two jackasses around the place were enough. Adding a four-legged one would be too much.

Safety regulations in the Thurber coal mines were inadequate and poorly enforced. The possibility of a cave-in was ever present. Pillars of unmined coal, plus beams and timbers, supported the earth above the miners, but the heavy overburden could snap the props at any

---

*I was at the neighboring Lyra coal mine in the early summer of 1945 when several donkeys were brought to the surface. Being blind from living underground so long, they were promptly shot.—Ed.

moment, causing a partial collapse of the ceiling. I learned about such dangers from young friends who began working in the mines at sixteen. These were chums who grew much faster than I did. We were all seven the year we started to school, but when I reached twelve, two or three had passed their sixteenth birthdays and had quit school to work in the mines. The company readily accepted the word of the parents or an entry in the family Bible to establish age. One such friend was killed when a powder keg exploded only a month or two after he started work. But men and boys entered those shafts to mine coal, not to cower before death traps round about them—and mine coal they did.

Coal mining in Thurber was closely geared to railroad demands. The number of passenger trains and their mileage was fixed, so coal consumption was relatively constant. The same was true of local freight trains. Switch engines covered about the same number of miles day after day. But the daily demand for coal could fluctuate as seasonal traffic changed. For example, cattle were moved to market each fall and winter, and sales influenced the size and movement of cattle trains. Fall and winter also were cotton picking and ginning seasons, which meant heavy shipments of cotton. Whatever the case, T&P officials calculated their coal needs with considerable accuracy. I never heard of a layoff or a speed-up at the mines because of miscalculations in coal demands.

Mingus was only one of the many coaling points on the T&P, but the activity at the coal chutes was predictable. Each day, switch engines pushed five or six cars of coal on the chutes, and approximately two hundred tons poured into coal bins. This was a small amount when compared to the coal fed to the locomotive tenders at the railroad division points at Fort Worth and Marshall. Coal theft could occur at any station. The T&P in 1909 sent a young railroad yard clerk to Mingus to investigate coal theft. He found that a carload a day was disappearing through the manipulation of freight waybills at the depot and quickly stopped the thieving. Shortly thereafter, the station agent was transferred to Abilene, which at that time paid agents less than they were paid at Mingus. Years later, this yard clerk told me that the waybills at Mingus for cars of coal for a period of ten years averaged from 100 to 130 daily.

Thurber coal not only powered dozens of locomotives, it also fueled the engines that pumped life into the district. At its peak, Thurber had fourteen mines in production, and at each mine a coal-burning steam engine ran the machinery. At the company brick plant, coal was used to fire the rows of kilns and ovens. Coal fed the big boiler that operated the power and ice plant. In Thurber and

Mingus, residents carried in coal for everyday household heating and cooking.

Much of the coal used in Mingus came from the railroad yards. A hundred loaded coal cars were bumped around the switchyards each day, and coal spilled from every locomotive tender at the chutes. Teenage boys regularly scoured the tracks with gunnysacks, picking up coal spilled from cars and locomotives, and peddled it around Mingus. During the summer, they could get ten cents a sack, but during cold weather the price rose to twenty-five cents. If pickings were skimpy, they never hesitated to scramble atop a loaded coal car and roll off chunks. A large chunk from a three-foot vein would easily fill one sack. This was outright theft, but I never heard of a complaint filed against those who purloined coal in this manner.

Thurber, as a company-owned town, was virtually self-sufficient. Its chief function was to make a profit from coal mining, but to do so, it engaged in many supportive activities. It operated its own machine shops, where men repaired and fabricated almost every part needed to keep the equipment running. A corps of painters and carpenters kept the houses and buildings in repair and constructed new ones as needed. When the company started replacing frame store buildings and residences with brick, its masons drew on brick from company kilns. Tinsmiths, blacksmiths, and plumbers were on call to maintain the city water system.

The company relied on the T&P railroad shops at Mingus for rolling stock to transport its coal. Here the railroad employed 140 men to build wooden gondolas, repair all types of cars, and maintain the engines. All incoming freight billed to Thurber was set off at Mingus, then moved on to its destination by a switch engine. Outgoing freight from Thurber was hauled north to Mingus. Each town was indispensable to the other.

For years, Thurber brick provided a sizable second revenue for the coal company. Millions of bricks were burned in the dozen or more kilns. I passed by the plant in a buggy as a small boy and remember seeing half of the large hill behind the plant shaved down for clay to make brick. Soon thereafter, the company located another clay deposit in a hill a mile and a half away and constructed a railway to haul clay to the plant. An electric engine shuttled back and forth every day with a dozen cars. After 1917 the T&P piped in gas from the Ranger oil field to fire the kilns.

Thurber boasted thirty or more stores and shops, all built to serve company employees. The company never operated a wholesale business or attempted to sell dairy and bakery products in surrounding towns. It did sell ice wholesale to those who came to the plant and bought large blocks to peddle in their respective communities. And non-Thurber residents were always welcomed at the retail outlets and places of entertainment. But the town was designed, in both recreational and business units, to accommodate company employees "from cradle to grave." The hardware store could sell a family a cradle, supply furniture for the home through life, then provide a coffin, hearse, and cemetery lot at life's end.

The company built a two-story brick structure to house a drugstore on the first floor, and offices for company doctors and dentists on the second. The store was modern in every way, and had a large soda fountain, which featured ice cream manufactured from milk and cream produced at the company dairy. The manager kept musical instruments on display to add a touch of class. The pharmacy was large and well stocked because druggists in those days had to compound nearly every prescription written by a doctor. Contemporary patent medicines and cosmetics lined the shelves. The drugstore also offered hand-painted china, cut glass, and a variety of watches and other pieces of jewelry.

Occasionally, Dad clashed with a company doctor. One time he wrote a prescription for a sick Italian child, and the father took it to the company drugstore to be filled. The pharmacist was out and a doctor filled it. In handing the bottle to the father, he warned the man, "If you give this stuff to your child, it will kill him." Startled, the father got in his rig and galloped to Mingus to report what the doctor had said. Dad assured him that the contents of the bottle might kill the child, but his prescription would not. He rewrote the prescription and sent the man to the pharmacist in Mingus. The father left satisfied.

At this point, Dad decided to make a list of his own code names for the dozen drugs that appeared in 90 percent of his prescriptions and gave it to the Mingus pharmacist. Since none of the names appeared in the standard pharmacopoeia, company druggists dared not fill the prescriptions. This one unwise statement by a company doctor lost the company hundreds of dollars in prescriptions. Even in those days, professional competition could get rough.

Store managers were alert and efficient. The company meat market was kept clean and neat and was designed and equipped to provide quick service to its customers. On one occasion, when the local rat population got out of hand and a few made their way into the market, the manager imported a set of ferrets and turned them loose in the building after hours. The rats quickly vacated the premises. Managers also were profit-minded. My brother, Harry, reported that, while visiting the general store, he watched the manager marking the prices on new coffins. The company had bought the coffins wholesale at a flat ten dollars each, but the sale prices ranged from twenty to one hundred dollars per coffin. The price doubtless included use of the company hearse.

In spite of its best efforts to provide the residents every amenity of a regular town, the T&P failed in certain areas. It built no tennis courts, golf courses, or swimming pools. With no town pool, company employees often swam in ranch ponds or pools in creek beds. A local favorite was Rock Creek, halfway between Mingus and Strawn. It had a bed of flat sandstone, and the water was shallow, with only a few step-offs into deep water.

W. K. Gordon sent his two children, a son and a daughter, to Rock Creek with his secretary one afternoon for them to wade and swim. The secretary made himself comfortable on the creek bank, and the kids took to the water. The girl, who could not swim, began wading in the shallow water, and the boy drifted off some distance in search of deeper water for swimming. Suddenly, there was a scream from the girl. She had stepped into a hole and was frantically trying to save herself. As the child fought the water in desperation, the secretary fainted. By the time the brother rushed up, she had drowned.

Churches that practiced immersion also used creeks or rivers. The popular place in Mingus was a shallow hole just west of the point where the road to Strawn crossed Palo Pinto Creek. Here sins were washed away during the warm months of the year. Although daredevil boys took plunges into near-freezing creek holes during the winter, I never knew of candidates for baptism daring to endure the ordinance of baptism until the Lord had warmed the water for them. That may have been a reason why preachers held protracted revival meetings during the summer.

Gambling was found in every mining camp, and Thurber was no exception. It never had a "Celebrated Jumping Frog of Erath County," but it did stage celebrated "badger fights." These were usually held for a big shot Easterner on his first trip to the Southwest. A crowd assembled and the fighters were brought on the stage. One was a big, fierce-looking, heavily scarred bulldog; the opponent sat in a heavy box from which a long rope extended. As bets were made, the crowd hissed at the bulldog, inciting him to a fighting rage. When excitement had reached a peak, the guest of honor was handed the rope and told to give it a vicious jerk. This would place the "badger" in action. When the stranger gave a mighty tug, out of the box came the contender—a chamber pot rolling across the stage! A roar of laughter filled the air.

There was gambling aplenty in Thurber with cards, dice, games of chance, cockfights, and dogfights. One druggist in Mingus lost everything he had, including his drugstore, betting on roosters at Thurber's clandestine cockfights. He also left Dad holding the bag for about five thousand dollars in debts, secured by a mortgage on a nonexistent section of land in the Davis Mountains in West Texas.

My brother and I owned two Boston bull terriers, which a man named Matheson gave us. They were beautiful dogs and vicious fighters. One terrier, named Ted, would jump the fence every day and go down to the South Side Drug Store to enjoy free ice cream put out for him. One day on his return home, two big dogs attacked him. We saw the fight start and made a run for bats or clubs to help Ted out, but when we reached the front gate, the fight was over. Ted had whipped them both. Some two or three years later, we learned that Matheson had been shot to death. He was a professional gambler who bred, raised, and trained terriers for dogfights.

Thurber was a workingman's town. The men labored hard in the coalpits, played hard, and drank hard. Most of them did some betting or gambling of one form or another, winning part of the time and losing the rest of the time. The company owned them and their homes and directed their destinies. They lived in a unique world.

5.   Fun and Frolic

MINGUS COULD offer little in the realm of amusement and recreation when I was a boy. As a result, our fun and frolic was closely related to school, family, and social organizations. There were no opera houses, organized sports, or community parks. We still lived in the era of Confederate reunions, sterling family characters, and box suppers. It was a time of transition, when the individual still mattered.

I well remember the first picture show that came to Mingus. A Japanese couple got off the noon train one day, made arrangements to use the Woodmen of the World lodge room for the night, and circulated handbills advertising a moving picture show for the evening. Tickets were either five or ten cents. The only thing I remember about the picture was the jerky, soldierlike movements of the actors.

Four or five years later Mingus sported an open-air picture show. The owner enclosed a fifty-by-one-hundred-foot plot of ground with sheets of second-hand corrugated iron and erected a projection room on four large cedar posts. The audience sat on two-by-twelve-inch boards nailed to blocks that had been sunk in the ground. A large piece of white canvas served as the screen. At the end of a reel, a note flashed on the screen: "A Moment Please while the Operator Changes the Film." The pictures still flickered, but not as badly as those shown by the Japanese couple. I could not scrape up a dime regularly for admission, but I managed to see about half of the shows. The movie screen faced our backyard, and I soon learned that by climbing to the top of the fence and hanging on to a post for balance, I could see the top half of the picture.

After two or three summers, Gus Peterson opened the Mingus Theatre. Peterson's equipment was much better, but it was several years before projectors provided a continuous show. When the age of the serials arrived, the *Perils of Pauline*, starring Pearl White, was a favorite. Serials appeared twice a week, following the feature film. At the end of each episode, the villain would have Pauline tied across a track as a speeding express approached, or hanging from a cliff, or in some other type of peril. As the next episode opened, the hero showed up in the nick of time to prevent a tragedy. When Pauline was rescued, all hell would break loose in the movie house, as the spectators—men, women, boys, and girls—stomped their feet and gave off a medley of screams, rebel yells, hollering, and ear splitting whistles. This lasted for several minutes, but no part of the plot was lost, for we were still in the days of silent film. Aside from lodge and church meetings in Mingus, the picture show was the sole source of family entertainment outside the home. Peterson gave up the theater after the mines closed.

Menfolk fared a bit better for entertainment—at least some of them thought they did. In both Thurber and Mingus, customers gathered in saloons to fraternize and drink. Thurber also had clubrooms with billiards, nine pins or bowling, and many other recreational facilities. Mingus had pool halls and domino parlors, and about 1914, a Major Harwood, who ran a hardware store, started a skeet club. It was not exclusive. Anyone with a shotgun, a dollar for clay pigeons, and fifty or seventy-five cents for shotgun shells became a member for the afternoon shoot. In this way, Harwood increased sales at his store.

Tennis, golf, basketball, and football were all but unknown in Mingus at this time. Organized basketball may have been played in the Thurber public schools after 1915, but not in Mingus. Ferd Hill, a Mingus grocer, in some strange fashion discovered golf. He bought a driver and a few golf balls and began practicing in his Johnson grass field. He persuaded Father to buy a driver, and shortly thereafter the grocer and the doctor were hooking and slicing golf balls together. That is as near as golf ever came to Mingus. No one in Mingus, and few in Thurber, had ever seen a football game. However, footballs showed up at school each fall. At recess and at noon, we took the name of the game literally and applied the foot to the ball. The basic rule was to kick the hell out of the ball or, better still, kick the skin off the shin of the opposition. That was football in Mingus until the 1920s. Tennis might have been played in Thurber, but there was none in Mingus.

All the kids played baseball each spring. In the schools, both boys and girls participated, but the games were always segregated by sex. The girls used a black solid rubber ball about two inches in diameter and a bat fashioned from a bed slat or a one-by-four, with one end whittled down to where it could be easily grasped by the hands. They used no baseball mitts. Pitching to the batter was a slow, underhand delivery. In the case of a "hit," a fielder could register an "out" if she could retrieve the ball and toss it between the runner and the next base. Boys' equipment followed more conventional lines, but was inexpensive. Balls cost from fifteen to fifty cents each. Bats ranged to fifty cents. Mitts were thirty-five cents, with a quality catcher's mitt costing seventy-five cents. We had no uniforms, cleated shoes, chest protectors, or catcher's masks.

We lived in a world of make-do. A boy could dream for years for a $1.50 Daisy air rifle or a $3.50 tricycle, while a bicycle was beyond all hope. If someone wanted a bow and arrows or a kite, he made his own or did without. We fashioned Indian tepees and military tents out of gunnysacks. To build a car or wagon, we cut out two or four wooden wheels with a keyhole saw and attached them to wagon beds. Guns, swords, spears, Bowie knives, and shields also were made of wood and reflected the user's craftsmanship and imagination. If a boat was needed on the pump hole at the creek, we got some boards and built one, along with a man-powered motor, an oar.

We also learned to play croquet. Father and Mother and their friends liked to play croquet during the warm weather months when the moon was full. At times, they played until two or three o'clock in the morning—but would give me the devil if I came in after ten from a date. As there were no electric lights for the croquet court, a system was improvised for seeing the wickets at night. Dad would rip up an old bed sheet, wrap each wicket with a strip of cloth, then tie a big white bow at the top and in the middle. As a result, we could see the wickets from any point on the court. On the other hand, croquet balls were not easily seen and could be surreptitiously moved to a more favorable position between shots—or an opponent's ball could be "accidentally" kicked to an unfavorable lie. Such opportunities may have been a reason for the popularity of moonlight croquet playing.

Preachers in my youth described many things that could lead one astray. They usually included billiards, card games, forty-two, picture shows on Sunday, drinking malt or alcoholic beverages, entering saloons or pool halls, and on and on. Old John Dyer was thirsty one hot summer day after unloading a heavy load of freight from his dray and entered a saloon and ordered a schooner of beer. One of his Baptist brethren espied John in the act and charges were filed. The congregation met with an elected moderator and in convocation heard the charges. John Dyer admitted drinking the beer and told the group why. At this point the convocation forgot that it was a Baptist group and assumed the prerogative of a Catholic priest. If Brother John would say that he was sorry for having drunk a mug of beer, they were ready to absolve him of his sin. Otherwise, he would be thrown out of the church. John Dyer was no hypocrite. He got up and walked out and never again attended church after this brush with the local authorities.

Mother constantly reminded us of the gates to hell. She regarded it a cardinal sin to go to a picture show on Sunday, but saw no sin in spending ten hours on the Sabbath playing dominoes, forty-two, pitch, or other card games. She liked to play such games, but cared little about going to a Sunday picture show. Anyone who drank whiskey was on board a fast train for hell. Yet, there was always a bottle of whiskey in the kitchen pantry. She did not drink it, but used it to flavor mincemeat pies and enliven the eggnog at Thanksgiving and Christmas, and for toddies when she had a cold. She was subject to quite a few colds.

Of the many characters I knew as a kid, Grandpa Kindred Felts made the greatest impression. From the time I can first remember him, he changed very little in looks other than the last traces of red in his hair and beard turning white. His habits never changed. In my preschool years he frequently took me with him on trips lasting less than a day, and as I grew older sometimes for as long as two or three days.

Grandpa had been reared in northern Missouri. His family were slave owners and Southern sympathizers. When the Civil War divided the Union, he had no particular interest in joining either army until his mule was shot from under him one night while coming home after dark. His father advised him to join the Confederates for his own safety, and he followed the advice. Grandpa joined the forces commanded by Gen. Sterling Price.

When the war ended Grandpa returned home, hoping to return to the peaceful chores of farming and stock raising. He soon learned that his damn-Yankee neighbors had other ideas. He possibly could have joined the renegade James and Younger brothers, but instead he decided to move his family to Texas. Grandpa settled first in the West Cross Timbers, where he farmed and horse traded for some thirty-five years, then sold his farm and moved to Mingus just across the street from our place.

After Grandpa sold his farm and moved to town, he had a lot of time on his hands. He would shuck corn to feed Chick twice a day and throw him a block or two of Johnson grass hay. Chick was his horse and Chick did very little to earn his oats. He was hitched up on occasion to haul Grandpa and the buggy to a Confederate soldier reunion, or for a jog to the creek to catch a mess of perch. As a result of inactivity, Chick weighed enough for two ordinary horses.

To while away time, Grandpa took a nap in the morning and another one in the afternoon. He and Grandma played dominoes quite often, but the thing he seemed to enjoy most was having her read to him. He did not take much stock in the Bible, but the *Stephenville Tribune* came each Saturday, and she had to read every word of it. He wanted to keep up with his old Erath County friends. His steady reading diet was *The Story of Cole Younger*, a paperback autobiography he had purchased from a train news butch.

It was a good show to watch Grandpa while Grandma read the story of Cole Younger to him. He would fill, tamp, and light his clay pipe, which had a stem cut from a length of bamboo, then settle back in his cane-bottomed chair and gently puff away as Grandma read. While the story flowed he usually hooked his heels over the bottom rung of his chair and tilted back against the wall, resting his head. Years after his death there was still a black spot on the wall built up over the years by oil from his hair. But when the Younger story filled with action, all four legs of his chair hit the floor, he would lean forward, elbows on knees, eyes flashing and in rapt attention. Grandma's reading had its own eccentricities. "It" was always "lit" and "are" was never anything but "air," and she had her own pronunciation for other words.

Grandpa had heard *Cole Younger* read so many times that I am sure he could have recited it from memory. But his interest in each rereading never varied. The reading sessions were never interrupted for idle conversation. To him, the gospel according to Cole Younger was just as sacred as was Bible reading to a circuit-riding preacher. I found the old book many years later while rummaging through some of his things and saw that the outer pages were worn black from the countless thumbings. ·

As a lad, we could purchase all the fishing gear we needed for fifty cents. A dozen hooks cost a dime, while another dime would buy fifty feet of fishing line. And a bamboo pole, depending on its length, came to fifteen or twenty-five cents. We pulled corks from bottles about home and used them for bobbers. If we could not locate a piece of lead in the house or the shed, we removed the lead nose of a 22-calibre rifle shell with a pair of pliers, hammered it to paper thinness, and wrapped it around the fishline just above the hook. This was a great sinker. With a tin can and a grubbing hoe, we could dig in some damp earth and find a can full of worms for bait. A tow sack, with a string to keep it tied shut, and long enough to anchor it to the creek bank, kept our fish catch alive.

With a little work, we could make a dip net that would guarantee a supply of minnows for bait. The net was made from a piece of discarded window screen about two feet square. We stitched this to some heavy wire bent to shape a square about two feet, allowing a slight sag in center. A small piece of screen, about four inches square, was cupped slightly and stitched to the middle of the big screen on opposite sides. In this pocket we inserted a piece of bread to attract minnows when the net was placed underwater. We attached a cord to each corner, knotted them together about a foot from the net, and tied a single cord to the knot. Grasping the cord, we could lift the net from the water whenever we needed a fresh minnow. Surplus minnows from the net were dumped into a pail of water kept nearby.

Some fishermen preferred frogs or grasshopper bait. A stiff branch, three or four feet long, with a thick bunch of leaves at one end made a good trap for frogs along the bank or grasshoppers in the grass. The all-purpose jackknife, which every boy owned, rounded out the essentials for any fisherman. Some disciples of Izaak Walton probably preferred half a dozen throw lines anchored to the bank or trotlines to pole fishing.

I was twelve before I saw an artificial lure. I was fishing at the Mingus Lake, half a mile west of town, when I saw Mart Smith poking a long bamboo pole in the roots and brush along the edge of the water. When he reached me, I noticed that the pole had a three-foot line dangling from the end, and a bright lure attached to the line. Smith had been trying to snag a bass from among the roots, and he must have been successful for a three-pound bass was hanging from his belt.

Besides hunting and fishing to ease life's burdens and cares, we had town picnics. The country around Thurber and Mingus still had a few former Confederate soldiers and an occasional "damn Yankee" when I was a kid. Bill Heath, the Mingus postmaster until Woodrow Wilson became president, was the only known Republican in town who was not a Northern veteran of the Civil War. Once or twice a year there was a picnic for the Confederate veterans. Always present, wearing gray uniform and black military hat, often on horseback and sitting broomstick straight was decorous Colonel Sawyer from Thurber. Grandpa Felts swore that Sawyer had been a buck private who promoted himself periodically after the war until he attained the rank of colonel.

At the other end of the spectrum was Captain Russell. Russell was an old bachelor who lived outside of town. He was a fine man but often would have a little too much to drink on his infrequent visits to Mingus. When under the influence of John Barleycorn, he would recite his war history, which went something like this: "I am James Junior Russell (never James Russell, Jr.) from Flat Creek, Virginia, by God, a member of Lee's Army of Northern Virginia (followed by division, regiment, and company identifications, which I have forgotten), the sorriest man in the company, but they elected me captain, by God. I wasn't more than a hundred yards from General Lee when he surrendered at Appomattox Court House." If a sympathetic audience plied questions, Captain Russell would fill in detail after detail, but the introductory speech never varied.

During the morning the veterans handed down cane-bottomed chairs from the wagons and collected in a group. They sat around puffing clay, corncob, briar, and perhaps a rare meerschaum pipe, smoking Whale tobacco at fifty cents a pound, telling anew the tales and experiences of the war. I am sorry that I never had time to listen to them. If I had, I would have heard enough Civil War tales to have written about for another fifty years. But I was too busy playing with the "young 'uns" to mess around with the "has beens." While the old men talked, the women visited with each other and emptied baskets of food on temporary tables of boards laid across sawhorses.

The afternoons were usually given to speechmaking. Picnickers paid rapt attention as orators lauded the righteousness of the Lost Cause, covered its leaders with laurels, and praised the heroism and bravery of its men and women. Formalities were closed by a band playing "Dixie." Rebel yells filled the air as clouds of Stetson hats were tossed on high again and again. By 1920 the ranks of Gray had grown too thin for such celebrations. American Legion halls were then filling in where gatherings of Confederate veterans had left off.

Local churches and lodges annually sponsored ice cream and box suppers, but only the churches had Christmas parties. In Mingus there were several denominations, but the Baptists and Methodists monopolized these affairs, rotating yearly with each other. A large cedar tree, cut in the nearby hills, was set up in the church building, and kids loaded it with green and red tallow candles and yards of tinsel, and wrapped red and green paper ropes around and up and down the tree. Occasionally, a large tinfoil star was placed on top. A few families put family gifts on the tree, but we never did. As kids, we went primarily for the program and the candy.

After a medley of Christmas songs, readings, and stories, Santa made his entrance dressed in a red suit, with a bag of toys over his shoulder. He was ringing a cowbell or a brass classroom bell and ho! ho! hoing to a fare-thee-well. Santa was always a member of the Sunday school or some local layman. The last year I spent at home, it fell my lot to be Santa. In trying to disguise my voice, I fell into a black dialect and drew a lot of ribbing as a result.

When Santa began calling out names, the kids became excited and so did Bill Wilhelm, the only black ever tolerated in Mingus by the town's Great White Fathers. Bill always got two or three presents, so he sat on the edge of a pew, ready to respond. When his name was called, he rushed down the aisle yelling all the way, "Heah, heah, heah, heah." Whether the Baptist or Methodist churches ever filled during the year, I do not know, but they were generally overflowing on Christmas tree night.

Ice cream suppers were held during the summer. The Missionary Society or Ladies Aid Society sponsored these affairs to raise money to buy needed hymnbooks, church pews, or a new Bible for the pulpit. The suppers were well advertised. The congregation furnished ice cream freezers, milk, cream, eggs, sugar, available fresh fruits, and flavorings. Nothing was bought except ice and salt. The men spent the afternoon freezing a variety of flavors then packed each freezer with chopped ice and salt to keep the cream firm.

We had two hand-cranked freezers, a one-gallon size and a three-gallon. Both were always borrowed. The three-gallon was seldom used at home, unless there was a gathering of the clan. As the freezer can tended to rust between uses, the last ice cream supper it served was costly. The person who took the first bowl blew a mouthful of cream halfway across the yard, sputtering, "S . . . A . . . L . . . T!" The abrasive action of the ice and salt had worn away the rust on the can, making holes. The three-gallon can of ice cream had filled with salt water.

Box suppers were more fun than ice cream socials. Women and girls spent as much time decorating their boxes as they did in preparing the food that filled them. St. Valentine's Day was a favorite time for some organization to sponsor a supper. Boxes were covered with red and white crepe paper, garnished with homemade hearts and cupids, and bound with ribbons of the same color topped off with large bows. Yet a fellow could get badly stung if he bid only on the attractiveness of the box. Some gals took a plain shoe box and filled it with three or four biscuits, several pieces of fried chicken, and slices of delicious pound cake, and tied the lid with wrapping string. Husbands usually recognized the boxes their wives prepared and in their bidding turned to others for partners.

The real excitement at a box supper centered on the bidding for boxes of unmarried women. Boys and young men studied the boxes, pretty or otherwise, and the contest went fast and furious when two or more wished to eat with a particular girl. The trick was to know the box the favored girl brought. Sometimes this was difficult. When a boy bought the wrong box, you might see the victim choking down his food while trying to carry on a conversation with the girl in monosyllables or not at all. The worst happened when the fellow failed to recognize the box of the girl he was sweet on. He would be ribbed about it for days, and his girl would give him the ice treatment for a while.

At one supper, a blonde two or three years my senior who lived across the street brought a beautiful box. To her I was a kid in knee britches, but to me she was my girl even if she was dating young men. When the auctioneer lifted her box for bids, I opened with fifty cents. One of her boyfriends immediately bid seventy-five, I went to $1.00, he bid $1.25, I raised to $1.75 and he did not bid again. All the poor chap had was $1.50. I had not a penny, but John Thomas Spratt, my banker, was sitting across the hall and fished out the money, telling me that I could have had the box for twenty-five cents less.

Family visits were also interesting events. These get-togethers generally occurred on Sundays and included two families, although three or even more were not unusual. Sometimes, the families were related, but most of the time they were merely good friends. Two or three families could easily bring together a dozen or more people of varying ages. This gave the men an opportunity to iron out political and economic problems that, at Mingus and Thurber, usually hinged on the railroad and the mines. The women had a chance to exchange recipes and the latest gossip, while the kids spent the day playing every game they knew.

The main event of the day was the noon meal. The women loaded the table with fried chicken and several kinds of meat, cream gravy, mashed potatoes, cooked vegetables, preserves, hot biscuits, butter, coffee, tea, sweet or buttermilk, and, in season, fresh onions, radishes, tomatoes, and fruit salad. Home canned peaches or home baked cake served as dessert. With a dozen or more to be fed, there was a first table and a second table. The kids had to wait for the second table. The first table always filled with the biggest gluttons and wind-jammers in the country. They could eat and blab and blab and eat forever. A call for the second table seemed to take hours. After the dishwashing had finished for both tables, the kids headed back for more play, while the adults turned to dominoes or forty-two. Visits could last for some time, and if the visitors came from a distance of twenty miles or more, they spent the night, with pallets spread throughout the house.

As the afternoon grew late, the men would harness their horses to the buggies, surreys, or wagons; the women would round up the kids; and the families headed for home. By the late 1920s this tradition of family visiting was ending in Mingus. It had been killed by the telephone, the automobile, and radio.

6. Rare Events and Big Celebrations

T HE CHAUTAUQUA movement, well known for its dedication to enriching the cultural life and broadening the educational base of American towns, failed to strike roots in either Thurber or Mingus. This was strange, considering that the combined population of the two communities ranged between ten thousand and thirteen thousand during the early decades of the century. However, Chautauqua management may have written off coal towns and small railroad towns as beyond the ken of civilization, or, they may have been rebuffed when they offered to include either Thurber or Mingus in a summer schedule. The T&P management may have thought that local families already had adequate enrichment programs, so why underwrite a Chautauqua guarantee? Mingus had neither a Chamber of Commerce nor a merchant association, and in the absence of such organizations it was impossible to secure an agreement that would protect the Chautauqua against financial loss.

Yet both Thurber and Mingus enjoyed a broad range of cultural activities. A large number of families in Thurber probably had a deeper understanding and appreciation for music than most Chautauqua musicians who moved about the country as ambassadors of good music. Italians formed the largest non-Anglo group in Thurber, and it was generally felt that they ranked near the top among the peoples of the world in their knowledge and love of music. Many played in the Thurber band, which drew large crowds for its regular Sunday evening concerts in the bandstand on the square. The band won wide acclaim and many awards for its fine music.

Nor was Thurber without artists. One of the Italian miners who came to Thurber directly from Rome was a painter. Luigi was his given name, but I do not recall the surname. Given the use of a vacant store building in Mingus, he painted a picture of Christ that graced the Catholic church in Thurber for many years. Later, it became part of the Vatican art collection. Universal Pictures learned of Luigi's work, liked the imagination he displayed, and induced him to come to Hollywood at a salary of twelve thousand dollars per year as its scenery artist. Later Metro-Goldwyn-Mayer took him into their studios at a salary of $25,000. Music and painting were only two of the talents that flourished amidst the coal dust of a mining town.

Circus performances were rare treats when I was a kid. The large shows arrived by rail in a long train that included dining cars, bunk cars for the roustabouts, pullmans for the stars, plus a private car for the owner. Smaller shows moved in condensed form. They leased or owned one or two pullman coaches, and carried tents, wagons, and animals on two or more boxcars and flatcars.

The Mollie A. Bailey Circus regularly stopped in Mingus on its annual tour. Mollie's pullman displayed large red and gold letters that advertised the MOLLIE A. BAILEY CIRCUS. Rendered in circus script, the sign stretched the length of the car and filled the space beneath the windows. As I recall, Mollie Bailey was a native of Mississippi. She and her husband had run the circus until his death, and she now carried on. Her show traveled the southern states, but it put on most of its performances in Texas towns.

Mollie was known as the "Darling of the Confederate Veterans" and seldom missed one of their reunions. At these affairs, when she came to the rostrum she was royally welcomed by the best rebel yelling the old boys could muster. For one reason or another, Texas became a haven for ex-Confederate soldiers. There were enough of the Boys in Gray in every community, along with their families, to fill Mollie's tent every time her circus dropped in for its one-ring, one-night stand. In all the years her circus came to Mingus, she never failed to have a full tent. Grandpa Felts would have gotten out of his deathbed to see her show one more time if he knew it was in town.

Only once did a three-ring circus gamble on Thurber-Mingus as a profitable stop. About 1915 the side of every barn in our area blossomed with colorful billboards announcing that the Sells Floto Circus would be in Mingus for two performances. This circus had its own trains. Excitement grew as the circus date drew nearer. Where would people come from to fill the big tent twice in one day? Where would the circus find room to spread its tent city? Who would furnish water for the animals and the circus people?

It was decided that the so-called courthouse square, a block north of the railroad, could serve as a circus lot for a day. When the roustabouts put up the tent city, it sprawled over most of the lot. Farmers appeared with loads of grain and hay for the animals, and the water pump at the Mingus Lake worked overtime. Advance men for the circus made ample provisions for food and other supplies and contacted

·workers at the railroad shops to stand by for servicing and making repairs on circus cars. Dad even took in a goodly number of fees for handling injuries to the circus crews and prescribing for other ailments. All who rendered a service to the circus were paid in cash and received complimentary show passes.

Both the matinee and the evening performances played before full tents. People poured in from the neighboring towns of Thurber, Strawn, Gordon, and Mineral City, and from farms as far out as twenty miles. Never before or afterward did so many people gather in Mingus on one day for a single event. Feeding such a crowd could have posed a problem, but families were still accustomed to packing a box of food in buggies, surreys, or wagons, along with feed for the animals. Those who brought no food from home taxed the capabilities of the several restaurants in Mingus. Everybody came to the circus to have a good time, and they did. The Sells Floto Circus did well financially, and so did most of the merchants and workers in town.

One day John Kern drove up to his house across the street in the funniest buggy my brother and I had ever seen. The vehicle was a new rubber-tired model, but it lacked certain features. In the first place, it came rolling down the street without a horse or even a shaft for a horse. And the street did not slope enough for the vehicle to roll on its own. Furthermore, Kern was holding a stick that pointed down toward the buggy bed and was wriggling it back and forth from side to side. We thought he must have gone crazy because he was sitting on the left-hand side. Everybody drove a buggy from the right-hand side, for that was where the whipsocket was fastened to the dashboard. The buggy made a lot of noise, like it might suddenly fall apart. When Kern stopped at his front gate, we pulled our noses from openings between cypress pickets of the yard fence and ran to the house to tell Mother that Mr. Kern had just come home in a buggy without a horse.

Having been informed that we had just seen our first automobile (the year was 1907 or 1908), we headed across the street to inspect the new marvel. We drank in every detail while circling the contraption three or four times at what we considered a safe distance. Kern saw us examining the car and came outside and asked us the silliest question any man ever asked two boys: "Would you chaps like to take a ride in it?" Would we? We would!

Mr. Kern went behind the machine and lifted the cover of what would have been the storage section of a real buggy. There we saw a small, upright gasoline engine, possibly of three horsepower, and a flywheel. He twisted a gadget here and there, then grasped the rim of the flywheel and gave it a quick jerk backwards. After two or three jerks, the engine began to pop and sputter, and the three of us climbed in. Mr. Kern grasped the steering rod, pushed a pedal or two, and away we went. This was my first horseless buggy ride.

I never heard whether John Kern built the car or not. He could have, because he was quite a craftsman. This may not have been the first automobile in Mingus and Thurber, but if there was an earlier one, it had been kept well hidden from me.

At the outset the automobile frightened both man and beast. I never saw anything throw fear into an animal as the early automobile did to the horse. Most of them, even the gentlest old dobbins, simply went berserk at the approach of a car, and the strongest and most skillful horsemen were hard-pressed to control the frantic animals. In 1914 Father traded our two horses and their harness, the family surrey, and his buggy to Bob Loflin as part payment for a Chevrolet 490 touring car. He gave a ninety-day note for the unpaid balance, then drove the car to the county seat at Palo Pinto to get a county license plate. (For a number of years, license plates were county, not state, issues.)

With the oil discovery at Ranger in 1917, Kit Hardy and Peggy Lynn each started a jitney (taxicab) service with Model T cars in Mingus. Lease hounds, oil-field workers, organizers of wildcat companies, buyers and sellers of oil, as well as gamblers and prostitutes got off the train in Mingus and all were in a hurry to reach points not served by the railroad. The taxi business flourished. Kit and Peggy knew the surrounding country for a radius of fifty miles and would deliver a fare anywhere he wanted to go. Licenses for the operation of jitneys were unheard of.

Five or six years after Mr. Kern drove his horseless buggy down the street, I saw my first airplane. It had been announced that a plane would land in the Thurber baseball park, so a group from Mingus went over. Hundreds of people filled the park and a hundred more gathered around outside. We all gazed skyward. Finally a simultaneous shout from scores of throats alerted the crowd with, "Here it comes!" Sure enough, in the distance you could see a dot much smaller than the size of a hand. The dot grew larger by the minute, and finally emerged as a large white box kite. On the underside were the enormous black letters, "F-O-W-L-E-R."* The contraption circled over the crowd a time or two, then landed inside the ball park.

---

*Robert G. Fowler, a former race car driver, lost out with his Cole Flyer in the cross-country air race sponsored by William Randolph Hearst in the summer of 1911. After the contest ended, he apparently flew east (Novem-

It was the first airplane in that country. A $25,000 prize had been offered by some individual or corporation for the first person to cross the country from ocean to ocean in an airplane. How much time it took, or how many stops were made, was immaterial. Fowler was after the prize. He was either financing his flight by landing at towns along his route, or was just interested in picking up extra money. His landing fee, depending on the size of the place, ranged from $1.00 to $500.00. The coal company at Thurber guaranteed Fowler a landing fee, then sold tickets at one dollar each for admission to the ball park. I had no dollar but found a plank missing in the park fence and wormed my way through it. The plane was resting near the center of the field and I headed straight to it.

For three or four years, or ever since I had known there was such a thing as an airplane, I had been trying to build one. I had nailed together every old board I could find around the place for the wings. There were usually four propellers, two on each side, made of shingles nailed together in the form of a cross. On each propeller tip was attached a paper windmill. This contraption I dragged into the street to wait for a good wind. Since the machine was called an airplane, surely it would be propelled by a gale. But my plane never flew. I wanted a close view of a real machine so I could remedy the defects in mine.

The biplane flown by Fowler was a flimsy thing. Two cloth-covered wings were attached to a number of wooden rods trussed into vertical position by a network of piano wires. There was no fuselage. A relatively small engine rested on the lower wing and it turned the two propellers by means of chain belts, driven by cogwheels on the motor. The propellers looked fragile. The pilot's seat rested on a framework extending out several feet in front of the lower wing. The controls were heavy piano wires attached to either end of a foot lever, something similar to a buggy singletree. A small horizontal, winglike part extended several feet in front of the pilot, undoubtedly to control height. A much smaller piece sat in a vertical position, no doubt for guiding.

Fowler talked with people surging about him. He was dressed like the most stylish automobile driver of the day, with a cap, a pair of goggles, a sport coat with large patch pockets and straplike strips sewn front and back, and a pair of large leather gauntlets. He stayed

ber 7, from El Paso), following the railroad and barnstorming to pay his way, eventually reaching Florida (Ruth M. Reinhold, *Sky Pioneering*, pp. 21–30).—Ed.

around for less than an hour, then cranked his motor by giving a sharp downward tug on one of the propellers, put a plug in each ear, pulled his goggles down over his eyes, donned his gauntlets, strapped himself to his seat, and took off.

On the eve of World War I, Mutt Marshall built an airplane in Mingus. Mutt was a train dispatcher who had been badly bitten by the flying bug. He bought a plane kit and had it shipped by rail to Mingus. When it arrived he hired John Dyer to haul it to the shade of a huge pecan tree in the center of a Johnson grass field that belonged to my Uncle Charlie Felts. It was summer and Mutt wanted a comfortable place to work on his plane. After several weeks, he had assembled the machine and invited the townspeople out to see the local boy become a bird. With a good-sized group of spectators watching, Mutt strained gasoline through a chamois skin into the tank and started the engine.

Mutt's flight was almost as short as the first successful run by the Wright Brothers. His plane took off, rose some sixty feet from the ground, then crumpled. Mutt escaped with only a few minor bruises, but his plane was completely demolished. However, he was luckier than Fowler, who failed to win the prize for the first cross-country flight. Fowler was killed when his plane crashed in Arizona. Mutt Marshall, after his plane crash, gave up his job as a dispatcher for a career in the air and became one of the earliest airmail pilots.

Every year all of Thurber flocked to the picnic park and pavilion near the baseball field for holiday celebrations. On July 4 there was a jubilant gathering to honor the signing of the Declaration of Independence. Then came Labor Day, with blue-collar (black-collar might have been more fitting) workers filling the grounds. The Labor Day celebration included Saturday, Sunday, and the first Monday of September. Everybody turned out for these affairs. Miners and their families, farm people, folks from neighboring towns, and coal company officials all gathered together. W. K. Gordon, T&P superintendent, rarely missed these massive picnics, and Mrs. Gordon was often with him, especially in the evenings.

Carnivals furnished the bulk of entertainment. The crowds flocked to a full array of sideshows filled with freaks, strange animals, and snake charmers. There also were black minstrel shows, games of chance, a shooting gallery, gadgets for testing skill or strength, and baseball booths with prizes for knocking dolls off pedestals or for hitting the trigger that dropped a black boy into a large vat of water. Barkers sold small buggy whips (I always bought one then later wished I had never heard of the thing when my parents used it when I violated one of the mandates circumscribing my daily actions).

Colored balloons, cotton candy, pink lemonade ("sweet as honey dew, and cold as ice could make it!"), and heaven only knows what else were hawked to the picnickers. Novitt & Hoffman, wholesale banana dealers from Mingus, regularly had peddlers on hand to profit from the crowds. Refreshment dealers of one sort or another were seen, in many cases the members of a local club. The pavilion became the activity center each night, as dancers and an orchestra performed before large crowds.

During these holidays, the company converted the electric motor-cars used at the brick plant to other uses. The hill being gouged down to supply clay was a mile or more east of the plant, and the track ran right by the southeast corner of the picnic grounds. The company decorated the cars in red, white, and blue bunting, placed two rows of seats in each, and covered them with awnings to serve as a sunshade and protection against contact with the overhead power line. From morning to night, these small trains ran back and forth between the brick plant and the hill, loaded with passengers who paid fifteen or twenty-five cents for the round trip. This was one of the most popular attractions of the holiday. I begged to ride one of these trains, but was never allowed to because of the assumed danger of possible electrocution.

As rains seldom fell at Thurber during July or September, the Texas sun blazed down on the picnic crowds in unobstructed fury. There were no trees on the picnic grounds, so the only escape from the searing heat was under the pavilion, at the minstrel show, or in a sideshow. The heat was good for business. People went to all of the shows in droves. Barrels of pink lemonade were consumed, along with thousands of bottles of cold soda pop. Malt and alcoholic beverages could not be sold, because the picnic grounds were located in dry Erath County.

I went to one sideshow to see Iko and Eko, two wild men who had been captured deep in the jungles of either Central or South America. This was the first time a member of their tribe had ever been seen outside the jungle. They were albinos and could see better at night than in the daylight. They were thick-lipped with pink eyes and hair just about the texture, kinkiness, and length of twelve-month wool on a Merino sheep. They were young men in their late teens or very early twenties and were said to be brothers.

A number of families who drove to Thurber for one of these three-day affairs came in surreys and wagons decorated with ribbons of gay colors. This was especially true on the Fourth of July. On July 2 we would drive the surrey to Rock Creek and scour and polish every inch of it from the fringed top down to the running gear. American flags were scarce in the hinterlands, but in Mingus Old Joe Abraham always had a supply of red, white, and blue buntings. Mother bought yards of each color and decorated our surrey, weaving the strands between the spokes of each wheel. She draped the same colors from the top, securely pinning the strips to the fringe. A big red, white, and blue bow was tied to the buggy whip. Other streams of color floated from the harness, and sometimes Mother tied a bow to the forelock of our horses, Ross or Gnat, depending on which one took us to the picnic. Mother always tried to outshine or, in this case, outdecorate, everyone else—and she usually did, even if she had to work us half the night.

It always fell my lot to accompany Grandpa Kindred Stricklin Felts, Mother's father, on these trips to the Thurber picnic—or on any other trip he made, unless I was in school. His old clay pipe was his constant companion and he said he needed me along to carry his matchbox. That box contained about two dozen matches and doubtless was too much for him to handle. Anyway, it was convenient to have a boy hand him a match to relight when his pipe went out. For some strange reason, my younger brother, Harry, never grew in stature sufficient for Kindred to trust him with the matches.

For the trip to Thurber, he called for his best bib and tucker. This consisted of a black suit, a freshly laundered white shirt, a broad-brimmed gray Stetson, and a black string tie. His shoes he usually "blacked" the evening before. The clay pipe was put aside for a shiny briar with a big bowl. He took his watch from the nail where it hung by the old "eight-day clock" and slipped the plaited black kangaroo band over his head. This was his watch chain. He was then ready for a picnic, church, funeral, reunion, circus, or whatever.

Grandpa Felts always wanted to get an early start for the two-mile drive to Thurber for the Fourth of July picnic. I was never able to determine the reason for this. He might have been anxious to get there early; or, perhaps he wanted to be sure to see Confederate cronies whom he had not seen for several years. Or, he looked forward to visiting with the only "damn Yankee" he ever really liked. The two had been in one battle, on opposite sides, and they would spend hours recounting the details and sorting out where each was located during the fighting. They would repeat how much they now thought of each other, but quickly added that they sure as hell would have shot to kill if they had met on the battlefield. As each considered himself a dead shot, they both would have dropped dead in the exchange. Grandpa Felts hated Yankees, always recalling how he and a dozen of his war buddies "decorated" the trees around a Missouri courthouse one night in 1870, just a few minutes before they started their wagons and families across Missouri in a southwesterly direction for Texas.

In comparison to the holiday picnics in Thurber, the public entertainment in Mingus was less impressive. Occasionally, the wagons of a dog and pony show might stop for a one-night performance and usually played to a full house. With less frequency came stock companies with their repertoire of melodramas. They presented the favorite melodrama of the Bible Belt for those years, *Ten Nights in a Bar-room*, and in conclusion showed a stage alive with all of the reptiles and dragons that tormented the mind and soul of the depraved victim. On rare occasions a merry-go-round or carousel stopped in town and set up for business on the vacant lot east of the bank. It would stay around for a week or a month, depending on how long it took to drain the community of nickels and dimes. The town ruffians would nearly drive the owner and the town constable to distraction, hopping on and off the merry-go-round while it was in motion.

Once or twice a master daredevil brought his balloon to Mingus. His act was always exciting. While his balloon filled with hot air, the daredevil checked the parachute and trapeze on which he would perform. Picking several men to hold the ropes attached to the bag, he climbed aboard, stripped off his dirty work clothes and tied them to the trapeze bar. The tights he wore were about as grimy as his outer garments. All in readiness, he ordered the ropes released and up the balloon went. As it rose higher and higher, he performed various acrobatics on the bar. When the balloon reached its highest point, there was a loud gasp from the crowd, as the daredevil cut loose from the balloon and fell until the parachute neared the earth. A guy like that just had to have more guts than brains.

Thurber had no competition when it came to the social event of the year. This was the company's Annual (annual ball) given on New Year's Eve. It was strictly a black-tie, evening dress affair, and by invitation only. Many of the socially elite of Fort Worth and Dallas reportedly attended,* as well as several officials from the New York offices. These annuals stimulated conversation and conjecture for

---

*Contrary to popular belief, Wallis Warfield Simpson (who married Edward, Prince of Wales, in 1936) was never part of the social scene in Thurber. Coal mine No. 9 was named "Warfield" for Mary Warfield Ward, a cousin of Wallis Warfield. This may be the basis for the tale that Wally was in Thurber. William Hunter McLean (*From Ayer to Thurber: Three Hunter Brothers and the Winning of the West*, pp. 37–38) permanently buries the myth. Also see Gentry, "Thurber," p. 24.

months before and after. There probably was more talk about the Annual among those who never attended these dances than there was among those who did. When local Protestant ministers exhausted their sermon topics, they invariably speculated on the sins stemming from the Annual. Some people made remarks out of envy and jealousy, while others were proud that such a social affair was held in their town. The Thurber Annual certainly was not an event ordinarily associated with the social life of a coal mining community.

Four generations of Spratts, 1930: John Thomas, *rear; from left,* John S.,
John S., Jr., and John T., M.D. *J. S. Spratt Collection*

Louisa Felts and her parents, Kindred and Martha Felts, in front of the Felts home. *Courtesy J. S. Spratt, Jr.*

Kindred Felts in Mingus State Bank. *J. S. Spratt Collection*

Dr. J. T. Spratt on his horse Gnat in front of the Spratt Home. *J. S. Spratt Collection*

Dr. J. T. Spratt and his first automobile. *J. S. Spratt Collection*

Dr. J. T. Spratt's saddlebags, medical instrument case, and 41-calibre Colt revolver. *Courtesy J. S. Spratt, Jr.*

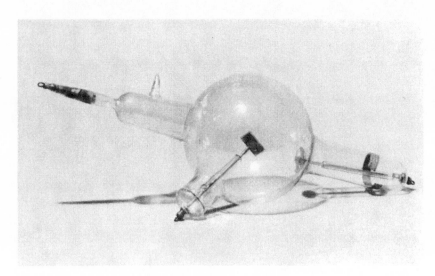

X-ray tube used in Dr. J. T. Spratt's office in Mingus; this is the first X-ray tube used in Pecos and Mingus. *Courtesy J. S. Spratt, Jr.*

THE THURBER JOURNAL.

Vol. VII.—No. 82.   THURBER, TEXAS: SATURDAY, DECEMBER 13, 1902.   WHOLE No. 334.

THE GREAT CHRISTMAS STORE

TEEMING WITH BARGAINS

XMAS SHOPPING IS MADE EASY AT THE T. P. M. & M. CO.'S BUSY DRUG STORE

There is not much time for you to stop and think now—the days are flying fast, and so are the Holiday Goods. "Ah, that pretty little bronze figure

XMAS SHOPPING IS MADE EASY AT THE T. P. M. & M. CO.'S BUSY DRUG STORE

I saw a few days ago is gone!" said one of our lady customers a few days ago. Yes, other rare things will be gone if you delay your shopping during these busy times, then you will find it too late to get more like them. Why wait? Why stop? Why think? No risk; never any risk to buy here—money back, if you wish. And if you don't know what to give—well, what can help you more than seeing the thousand and one things here? Christmas shopping is easy if you go to the T. P. M. & M. Co.'s Drug Store—EARLY!

ON FIRST FLOOR YOU'LL FIND

The most complete stock of Jewelry and Jewelry Novelties ever shown in Thurber. You can surely find a suitable Christmas Present from this big lot. Fine Watches, Diamonds, Rings, Buttons and Studs; SOLID SILVER Ebonized Toilet Sets, with Silver Ornaments; Ladies' Purses, with Silver and Bronze Tips; latest things in Chatelain Bags, in both Leather and Metal finish.

WE WERE ANTICIPATING A BIG TRADE FOR THIS SEASON, SO WE BOUGHT HEAVILY. OUR EXPECTATIONS WERE CORRECT—OUR TRADE IS GOOD!

ON FIRST FLOOR YOU'LL FIND

A most magnificent line of Meerschaum, French Brier and Fine Turkish Pipes, Tobacco Pouches, Plain and Fancy Match Boxes, Cigar and Traveling Cases, Combs, Nail, Teeth, Hair and Clothes Brushes, and a world of other appropriate Xmas Presents. Let us show you through the various lines on our first floor. Come early.

THEN, GO UP TO THE SECOND FLOOR
WHERE OLD SANTA CLAUS REIGNS SUPREME.

A tremendous line of Toys and Fancy Goods greets you—a line which we believe we are safe in saying is the largest and most complete to be found west of Fort Worth. They are selling like the proverbial "Hot Cake," too, and "you'll have to hurry" if you want first choice. Don't wait until the stock is broken, BUT COME NOW AND LET US SHOW YOU!

COME AND SEE FOR YOURSELF

I WOULD take a large amount of space to enumerate the various lines we are offering to the Holiday trade, so we will not attempt it. All we ask is that you come and see for yourself. We can show you better than we can tell you. KNOW WE CAN PLEASE YOU

For We Have Anything You Want!

FOR EVERY DOLLAR YOU SPEND

YOU get a chance at a magnificent FRENCH DOLL and A RUBBER-TIRED DOLL BUGGY, or, if you prefer, you can take a chance at the beautiful MEDALLION, worth $25. You can see the doll in our show window, or get a good look at "Fairy Dagny" at the head of the stairway, second floor. She is certainly a beauty, and you cannot afford to lose taking a chance to win her or the Doll and Buggy, so appropriate for your little daughter.

T. P. M. & M. CO.'S DRUG STORE.
THURBER, TEXAS.

Thurber Journal. J. S. Spratt Collection

Thurber, looking east. *Special Collections, University of Arizona Library*

Thurber, looking south from the hardware store. *Thurber Historical Association, Inc.*

Downtown Thurber, June 1917. *Special Collections, University of Arizona Library*

Thurber drugstore. *Special Collections, University of Arizona Library*

Thurber brick plant. *Special Collections, University of Arizona Library*

Italian miners, Thurber. *Thurber Historical Association, Inc.*

First State Bank, Mingus. *Courtesy Geneva Spratt*

Coal mine No. 10, Thurber. *Southwest Collection, Texas Tech University, Lubbock*

Thurber Opera House. *Courtesy J. S. Spratt, Jr.*

Black Diamond shuttle from Thurber to coal mines. *Special Collections, University of Arizona Library*

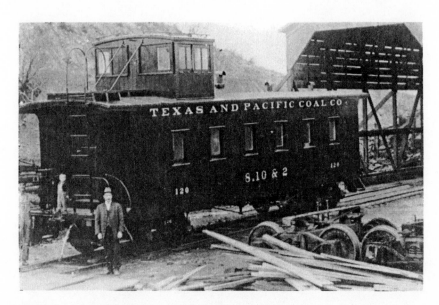

T&P car repair shop, Mingus. *Courtesy Geneva Spratt*

Horseshoe bar in Snake Saloon, Thurber. *Southwest Collection, Texas Tech University, Lubbock*

T&P depot, Mingus. *Courtesy Geneva Spratt*

Thurber families on a picnic. *Thurber Historical Association, Inc.*

Dr. J. S. Spratt, *left*, accepts check for Carr P. Collins Award in March 1956 for his book *The Road to Spindletop*; Collins, *center*, and J. Frank Dobie. *J. S. Spratt Collection*

7. The Local Business Scene

UNLIKE MOST Texans of that day, the residents of Thurber and Mingus were accustomed to handling cash and cash transactions in their everyday life. In both towns corporate payrolls injected cash into households to pay bills. Mingus may have had half a dozen farm families who lived with credit, but Thurber had none. Everyone paid in cash at the time of purchase, or at intervals of two weeks. In contrast, Gordon, their nearest neighbor, relied heavily on farm trade, which generally involved the annual settlement of debts. As a kid I became acquainted with the local business scene because of an early interest in the money world, a series of part-time jobs, and family involvements. It provided both an experience and an education for a boy interested in economics.

Twice each month I saw the westbound noon passenger train unload the Thurber payroll at Mingus. It arrived in a Wells Fargo express car and consisted of approximately $135,000 in currency locked in a company safe, plus eight or more large heavy canvas bags of silver dollars and other coins. A Texas & Pacific stagecoach, or taxi in later years, met the train. In staging days the driver had plenty of company. His guests rode horseback with carbines attached to their saddles and heavy-calibre six-shooters dangling at their waists. Their hats were broad-brimmed Stetsons. In appearance, these guards resembled a group of Texas Rangers, and they performed their assignments as efficiently and effectively as any Ranger unit ever did. While the payroll was being transferred from express car to company vehicle, the horsemen formed an aisle through which the precious cargo passed. When Bob, the driver, pointed his stage toward Thurber, he was encircled by these mounted guards. In Thurber another aisle was formed as the payroll was moved into the general offices of the coal company.

On one occasion, the train was held up and the express car robbed

a few miles east of Gordon.* The conductor immediately notified
the depot agent at Mingus, and the company guards headed east out
of Mingus at a gallop and quickly recovered the payroll intact. The
robbers had knocked the knob off the safe door, but had been unable
to open it before they were flushed by the guards.

Local merchants demanded cash. The company store in Thurber
never accepted payment in farm produce, but Mingus merchants occasionally settled in kind. Some grocers would take eggs, butter,
chickens, and turkeys, and possibly salt or smoked pork and smoked
hams. The lumberyard occasionally accepted livestock, especially
horses or mules, as partial payment on large bills. Oftentimes craftsmen, such as the blacksmith, tinsmith, and shoe cobbler, were par-
tially compensated with produce.

Few people in the Mingus-Thurber coal district in the early 1900s
were acquainted with banking or the investment world. A majority
of the townsfolk, especially in Mingus, had farmed, others had
worked at a trade, while most of the men in Thurber had been coal
miners either in this country or abroad. There were perhaps a dozen
professional men, but like my father they had spent their youth on
farms. The native-born inherited the old Populist fear of banks and
debts. Furthermore, local bankers had little experience in banking.
A majority had been successful merchants, ranchers, or farmers who
hired young men to serve as cashiers and keep books for them. These
young men had either learned the art from an old bookkeeper or had
attended a business college for three to six months to escape arduous
farm labor. As a consequence, few had much knowledge about money
and banking and viewed the operation as a simple process of lending
and collecting money. The banks at Mingus, Gordon, and Strawn
were founded by ranchers who let others run the bank while they
continued to devote their time to personal interests.

Mingus, Gordon, and Strawn never had a private banker, nor a
local man of means who regularly made sizable loans. Grandpa Felts
did some lending about town after he sold his farm in Erath County
and moved to Mingus. He was a fairly good judge of men, but his
loans seldom exceeded two hundred dollars. They were made to purchase a horse, cow, buggy, a hog or two, a new range for a restaurant,
or to a man for his wife's burial expenses. These were strictly character loans and were always repaid. He often extended the time period

---

*My grandmother, Mary Rebecca Johnson Abbott (1858–1943), lived on a
farm east of Gordon and remembered this train robbery at Judge Switch. She
said the engineer kept the whistle wide open all the way to Mingus.—Ed.

because he wanted interest on his money. After he passed fourscore years, his judgment slowed and Mother began supervising his loan business.

The bank in Mingus was chartered about 1910, and lasted for twenty years. It failed twice in that period. The first failure came as a result of business reversals after World War I. It survived that by means of the double-liability law, which made every bank stockholder, in the case of a bank failure, liable for a second full value of his stock. When the bottom dropped out of the stock market in the fall of 1929, the bank closed its doors for good. For its day, the Mingus bank had been fairly large, enjoying deposits of over $60,000 at one time.

The Mingus bank was typical of those found in small towns. Located in a two-story brick building, it sat on the southeast corner of downtown and was the most imposing structure in the community. Two persons usually handled its daily operations. An assistant transacted business at one of two teller windows, and the cashier sat in a section set apart at the front. He had a rolltop desk, a swivel chair, and two or three armchairs for customers. His office equipment included a typewriter, adding machine, and posting machine, but much of the work still was done with pen and ink. Several large bank calendars hung on the walls, the only decoration to be seen. The pictures varied from horse scenes to spots of natural interest. One year the bank set the town abuzz when customers unrolled its new calendar carrying a color picture called "September Morn."*

On the second floor Bearden & Cox rented one room to house the local telephone exchange when they installed the first telephone in Mingus. For a while, the other upstairs rooms were rented by Gus and Carrie Peterson, who ran picture shows in Thurber, Mingus, and Strawn. Downstairs, a back room, called the boardroom, ultimately became the post office.

The front of the bank developed into a social center. A porch covered with corrugated iron sheets extended out in front of the building and along the north side. This gave protection from both rain and sun. Plate glass windows on each side of the front door had low sills, which extended out about six inches. Here old-timers found convenient seats. If they grew tired of propping themselves against the

---

*This popular calendar depicted in color a nude young woman standing in ankle-deep water near a lakeshore on a crisp September morning. It was drawn by Paul Chabas circa 1912 (*Fine Art Reproductions of Old and Modern Masters*, p. 156).—Ed.

plate glass, they could sit on the sidewalk. Here they spun their yarns, straightened out the government, made crop forecasts, predicted the weather, decided who would be the best men for county offices in the coming election, wondered whether Old Man Jones would pull through this time or not, and what would happen to his widow if he did not. When the bank failed, the club disappeared.

The Mingus bank made small loans to local merchants and businessmen. For example, it easily financed blacksmith Hankins's purchase of a stock of horseshoes. The lot probably cost no more than a hundred dollars. The same was true of the tinsmith. The bank could lend Joe Abraham the money to pay for a carload of flour, and Novitt & Hoffman might even borrow one thousand dollars or fifteen hundred dollars to purchase a carload of bananas. The bank could lend Joe Teichman a few thousand dollars to finance the operation of his small flour mill.

However, the Mingus bank could not lend the Texas & Pacific Mercantile and Manufacturing Company $260,000 to meet its monthly payroll. In fact, it could not lend the company the money to pay for a month's supply of beer and whiskey—thirty carloads of beer and four of whiskey—for its Thurber saloons. It most certainly could not discount company bills for the sale of three thousand tons of coal, one day's sale. Nor could it have lent the company the funds necessary to finance a major expansion program. For such huge needs, the company dealt with large city banks.

Furthermore, many local people made no use of banks. Men carried cash in purses, and women kept household money in sugar bowls or empty baking powder cans. As people preferred silver and copper coins to pay bills, many utilized a black leather purse about three inches wide and six or eight inches long, with two pockets held shut by snaps. One side had a small pocket at the top; on the opposite side another pocket ran the full length of the purse and could store a large number of coins. As it was easy to wad two weeks' pay in old blackie, many men used these leather pocketbooks as depositories.

Like many boys, I spent considerable time in the Mingus drugstore. I watched the pharmacist work on his marble slab with spatulas, mixing and dividing various powders into prescribed doses, which he stuffed into capsules or folded into papers about the size of a cigarette paper. He also drew on rows of bottles, measuring and pouring designated amounts into graduated beakers. In those days, a druggist mixed and fixed 90 percent of all prescribed medicines, solids or liquids. Ready-prepared medicines were a rarity. Lydia E. Pinkham's Vegetable Compound was popular as an alcoholic beverage for women, being untainted by the curse of the saloon. Men bought Sloan's Liniment for both man and beast, and everyone leaned on aspirin for headaches. Asafoetida was in demand for fashioning medical amulets against contagious diseases, especially those causing high mortality rates. During the meningitis epidemic before World War I, half the people in Mingus wore bags of asafoetida around their necks as antiseptics or fetishes against the dreaded killer.

The drugstore also sported refreshments. On display were jars of jelly beans, gumdrops, sugar-stick (mostly peppermint), hoarhound, rock crystal (often saturated with whiskey for winter colds), licorice, and jawbreakers (what fun it was to suck on one for a time and then take it out to see what color was showing). And who could turn away from Wrigley's Juicy Fruit, Peppermint, and Doublemint *wax.* "Sody" pop (strawberry, vanilla, lemon, and root beer) came in bottles with permanent stoppers. To open the bottle, you gave the heavy wire loop a sharp downward push, which shoved the rubber stopper into the bottle and broke its seal. To close the bottle, the wire loop was pulled up until the stopper sealed tight. Regardless of the washing at the bottling works, the pop bottles were never sanitary.

But pop bottles probably were more sanitary than the medicine bottles used at the prescription counter. As families emptied these containers, they were oftentimes saved. I saw boys bring in a dozen to a hundred bottles in sacks, eager to collect one or two cents for each, depending on size. The bottles usually had been rinsed out, and if they looked reasonably clean they went directly to the prescription drawer. Father was still buying these used bottles for his drugstore in Mingus in the early 1920s. God alone knows how many, if any, deaths resulted from medicines taken from these second-hand bottles.

Everyone used tobacco. Drugstores sold various brands of cigars, but very few ready-rolled cigarettes. Smokers could buy burley twists, shave off a bit, and grind it between their palms to a fineness suitable for pipe or cigarette. Cut tobaccos came in one- or two-ounce bags or tins. Bull Durham, with its packet of cigarette papers, was far and away the favorite. A Bull Durham tag dangling by its yellow string from a sack inside a shirt or vest pocket was the badge of a "he man."

Garrett and Honest snuffs were popular among both men and women, and many homes depended on snuff glasses for drinking glasses. Most of the women were dippers, but men preferred to pull out the lower lip and pour a heaping teaspoonful into the pocket. This deposit generally lasted for several hours. Both pipes and chewing tobacco commanded a large following. Star Navy led the parade for those who preferred to chew. Plug tobaccos came in lengths of twelve inches, but every drugstore and grocery had a miniature guillotine to chop cuts of three, four, or six inches if the buyer wanted a smaller amount. Miners and Pubblers was the favorite cut among packaged chewing tobaccos. Chewing-tobacco guillotines were still around for years after World War I.

Operating the soda fountain at the Norwood Drug Store in Mingus was a full-time job. The syrup containers sat apart from the serving counter and in a cabinet against the wall. Each had a separate spigot. The soda jerk charged a glass of syrup with carbonated water piped to the fountain from a twenty-gallon water drum sitting on a cradle. To create carbonated water, one filled the drum three-fourths full of water, connected one end to the fountain and the other to a container of a carbonic gas, and opened the gas valve. The drum was rocked back and forth for ten or fifteen minutes on its cradle to mix gas and water. Closing the gas valve, you were ready to serve carbonated sodas, or ice cream sodas, to a thirsty customer.

Drums of gas came from Fort Worth by express. Ice cream came the same way. Five gallons of cream had to be left in the freezer buckets to keep it frozen. Every night, before closing time, an employee drained the water from the bucket and tamped ice around and over the top. Ice cream "combs" were popular with both kids and adults. People did not start buying ice cream *cones* until the 1920s. In my youth a nickel or dime would buy an ice cream cone, a soda pop, ice cream soda, or chocolate sundae.

As a doctor's son, I saw still another side of the local business scene. Townsfolk expected the local physician to handle all medical problems. He must diagnose illnesses, set broken bones, and clean and prescribe for major cuts and bruises. Babies came by home delivery, but the doctor was on hand to see that the newcomer made a safe arrival. When major surgery was necessary, patients were taken or sent to Fort Worth. Thurber had a dentist, but Mingus did not. As Father had a set of dental tools, he became adept at quickly killing the pain and extracting the offending tooth.

One young girl who was losing her baby teeth tried his patience. Dad seated Macie on his examination table, but before he touched the tooth, she cut loose and virtually kicked the office apart. Some time later when Macie came in again, he called Whitt Rosseau to hold her feet. Taking a halfway hold of each ankle, Whitt commented on what a docile child she was with not a kick in her system. Father warned Whitt to get a firm hold. When the instrument touched Macie's tooth, she came near to making Rosseau a toothless man. He then grabbed each of Macie's ankles in a viselike grip and mumbled,

"Now God-durn you, kick me if you can." The tooth came out without further damage.

Part of Father's office equipment was an indirect current generator. This was a huge machine that stood over six feet tall and was four feet wide and six or eight feet long. Its four glass sides encased a number of large glass discs attached to a common axle. Each glass wheel had a number of copper discs attached in such manner that these copper discs were brushed by series of small copper wires when the wheels were turned. A hand crank operated the machine.

The doctor could attach an ancient X-ray tube to the generator and with the aid of a fluoroscope (and me to crank the generator), he let papa or mama see the exact locale of the copper cent or the marble Jimmy had swallowed. People gazed in awe as they peered at the break in an arm, leg, or a badly damaged spinal column. One woman almost fainted when she was shown a 22-calibre bullet that her husband had been carrying in his skull for years. This probably was the only such machine in a doctor's office at that time between Fort Worth and Abilene.

The machine could produce amusing incidents, and I was present when one occurred. Dad used the machine to give electric treatments, and one day he had a woman seated in a chair with her feet resting on a lead plate for grounding the current. Above her head was a copper crown with a wire connection to the generator. As in many cases, I was turning the crank. Three or four of the patient's children, all under ten, were standing around to watch. While I was cranking away, one of them either reached to hand her something or to touch her, whereupon a jagged flash of electricity passed between the two. The kids thought this was funny and they all began reaching out to her to see the flash of the current. The mother tried to stop the electrical display by ordering them to stop, then resorted to physical means. She began to try to slap them. I was never really sure whether she was trying to slap the fire out of them, or whether the kids were trying to draw the fire out of her. Anyway, a beautiful miniature electrical storm filled the office for several minutes. The show was so comical that I kept cranking away. Dad never knew whether the electrical treatment helped the patient or not. He sold the generator in the 1920s.

As most early-day doctors never demanded payment before seeing a patient, they failed to receive regular compensation for their services. In one family Dad delivered babies through three generations without collecting a single fee. Other patients paid everybody else first and the doctor last. But people generally were honest and paid their debts, and small-town doctors lived in modest comfort.

Dad was a wise, practical physician. He became particularly interested in diseases of the lung, and everybody called him the best pneumonia doctor in that part of the country. During the World War I influenza epidemic, probably the deadliest of the century, he treated scores of flu patients in the Mingus-Thurber area without a single fatality. But a doctor could only go so far. On the eve of World War I, a meningitis epidemic swept through the country, and the medical profession seemed helpless. People drove doctors frantic with questions of how to escape the killer. Besieged with inquiries, Dad finally took a toothpick and punched four holes around a small white Bermuda onion. When questioned, he took the onion out of his pocket and held it for them to see. Soon those in Palo Pinto County who were not carrying a rabbit's foot or wearing a bag of asafoetida began carrying a Bermuda onion with four perforations.

In those days, family doctors and pastors were regular visitors in homes where there was a serious illness. Most families loved and respected these two servants of man more than anyone outside the immediate family. One day Brother Rucker, a Baptist minister, met Dad as he was leaving a home where a patient was seriously ill. They greeted each other, and Dad said, "Preacher, medical science has done all it can; if this patient lives, it is in your hands and those of the Lord's." When the minister volunteered to go in for a word of prayer, Dad went back in with him. They both knelt beside the bed to pray together that the Lord in his infinite wisdom would see fit to restore the sick to health.

John Thomas Spratt began his medical career with charges of fifty cents for an office call, one dollar for a day visit in town, and two dollars for a night call. For using the fluoroscope, he made no charge. Five dollars was his fee for setting broken arms, while broken legs ranged from ten to twenty-five dollars, depending on the nature of the break. There was a charge of thirty-five dollars for obstetric cases. Where there were prolonged sieges of pneumonia, typhoid, or other serious diseases, he usually added up his calls and halved the charge. For example, if he made thirty day and ten night calls in a pneumonia case, his total charges were twenty-five dollars.

As a family errand boy, I often visited Joe Abraham's grocery store in Mingus. Joe did well financially with his business. His store was twenty-five feet wide, with a covered porch on the front and a glass window on each side of the front door. From a side door about the middle of the building, he loaded his delivery truck. The interior arrangements were typical of that day. In the front part, a row of grocery shelves covered one wall from the floor to the ceiling. A moveable ladder attached to a rail was used to reach the top shelves.

Packaged items such as Arbuckle coffee, salt, pepper, and extracts stocked the shelves, along with buckets of lard and Cotelene, a type of shortening, and pails of honey and sorghum molasses. Canned goods were limited and canned preserves almost unknown. A counter paralleled the shelves, and tucked underneath were bins of dried fruits, dried beans (frijoles, lima, and navy), and cornmeal.

On the opposite wall, Joe had shelves filled with bolts of cloth, mostly ginghams and calicos, and a mixture of oilcloths, white and in patterns. He also carried rolls of unbleached domestic and linen. Once Mother sent me to Joe's for half a yard of linen. She cautioned me to test the cloth by placing a moistened finger under the cloth. If the moisture showed through immediately, it was linen, otherwise not. Blue denim rounded out the supply of soft goods.

Activity in the store centered on the counter. Here Joe measured and cut cloth and assembled customer purchases. Glass cases on the counter contained stick candies, gum and lemon drops, jawbreakers, and licorice. There were boxes of long, black, narrow and crooked cigars, which the miners liked, as well as chewing and smoking tobaccos and snuff. Nearby were hog jowls and sides of salt pork in a screened case. Here also was a cheese table, with a large round cheese enclosed in a wire cage to keep out flies. By means of a lever underneath the table, one could click off the desired amount of cheese, each click measuring four ounces, and cut the wedge with a large square knife attached to a hinge. Joe served many a hungry man a ten-cent wedge of cheese and a nickel's worth of crackers.

Virtually all of Joe's sales were on fifteen- or thirty-day credit. He filed a copy of each sales slip behind a spring clip attached to a metal sheet two feet square. Fifteen or twenty of these sheets were hinged to a metal container, with each sheet serving fifteen or twenty customers on each side. Joe noted on each slip the previous balance, new sales, and the new total. By this arrangement, he could quickly tell a customer his total purchases for the month or fortnight. Under this file was his cash drawer.

Walking toward the back of the store, one passed pickles, salted fish, vinegar, lard, peaberry coffee, and crackers. And just outside the service door stood a barrel of coal oil. Everybody bought coal oil for lamps and starting fires. When a customer presented a gallon can, Joe unscrewed the small potato jammed on the spout and pumped the oil to fill the order. We always used a five-gallon can and paid seventy-five cents for a full container.

The rear half of Joe's store served as a warehouse. Here he stacked hundred-pound sacks of bran for cow feed, hundred-pound sacks of chops for poultry, hog and horse feed, plus flour, cornmeal, sugar, and other items. Sacks of potatoes and dried onions and a few cases of ax handles, garden hoes, and rakes filled out the warehouse space. Joe occasionally offered special produce. As long as Novitt & Hoffman ran a wholesale banana business, he had a stalk of bananas in the store. At Christmas, there were coconuts, English walnuts, Brazil nuts ("niggertoes"), and hazelnuts. Oranges were seasonal, but lemons were around most of the year.

In contrast to Joe Abraham's operation in Mingus, the company grocery at Thurber ordered merchandise by carloads. Feeding a population of ten thousand required a small freight train of groceries each week. As the company had a huge cold-storage vault for its meat market, the grocery also used these facilities for storing fresh fruits and vegetables. But customers had few choices of staples in the company store; nor were bolts of cloth and oilcloth, needles, thread, and the like sold there.

The most famous peddler in Mingus was Anne Dow. "Old Peddler Anne," as we knew her, made her rounds every month or so, walking and hawking from Weatherford to Pecos with two large gray valises, one balanced on her head or shoulder and the other toted by hand. The goods and gadgets she stashed in those two grips staggered the imagination. Many housewives bought notions from the peddler because they felt sorry for her. They need not have, because that old Assyrian woman carried a shrewd business head on her shoulders. She and those two old valises accumulated the basic capital that she and her son John ultimately used to build a small frame store halfway between Mingus and Thurber and garner a modest fortune.

Both Thurber and Mingus had dry goods stores. The company store at Thurber and the two stores in Mingus were similar in their operations. The Thurber store was the largest and boasted a sizable supply of clothing for men. All three stores carried piece goods, as women still made most of the garments they wore. A wide assortment of laces were displayed, too, for lace embellished all their undergarments. As women sewed a great deal, practically every household had a sewing machine. Brogans, everyday shoes for men and boys, sold for about two dollars a pair. One pair of dress (Sunday) shoes sufficed for men, women, boys, or girls. Since dresses covered each woman's calf or ankle, they regularly wore lisle stockings.

Dry goods stores carried very little ready-made clothing. Suits occasionally were seen, but there were few dresses. Men could find an ample supply of overalls, and boys' knickerbockers were sold until they went out of style just before World War I. Dress shirts had stiff collars attached by two collar buttons. Collars ranged in height from one to two and a half or three inches tall and were made to accommodate long, medium, or short-necked men. The stores stocked hats and caps for men and boys, along with hats and bonnets for women and girls.

The only clothing I wore that came from the store was overalls and brogan shoes plus stockings. Mother ripped up Dad's old trousers and made them into boy's pants. She also made all of our shirts. I was twelve years old before I owned a store-bought suit—a coat with matching knickers. It made Mother angry when Dad bought me a pair of long trousers, and she promptly cut them off and made knickers out of them. Like most of the kids in town, I wore underwear made from American Beauty flour sacks, with their distinctive red rose. I never knew there was any other kind of underwear until I was a teenager. The big red rose always ended up on the flap of my drawers, and there it shone until they were threadbare, regardless of the washings and boilings they had.

The dry goods stores frequently advertised their wares. The company store at Thurber had sales, but I never saw one of their dodgers. In Mingus, both I. A. Fine and H. Samson pushed sales in their respective stores twice a year. For such events they either drove a buggy through the country spreading sales dodgers among the farm population, or they hired others to spread the news. Fine had no advertised business slogan, but Samson used "Samson sells it for less." They invariably marked goods up 20 percent for the sale, instead of reducing prices.

Fine once staged a promotion by offering prizes. The top prize was a table model, hand-cranked phonograph with a dozen records. Dad won the phonograph and records, and for years afterwards, with our house opened wide on summer evenings, the whole town could hear the phonograph blaring "Dixie," "Pony Boy," "Uncle Josh at the Bug House," "The Arkansas Traveler," and others.

It was a red-letter day in Mingus when the Brown Shoe Company sent Buster Brown and Tige to put on a performance in front of I. A. Fine's store, the local outlet for Buster Brown shoes. On one occasion, Tige became a little stubborn during the performance and Buster Brown took his cane, which was about eighteen inches long, and gave the dog two or three whacks across the rear. Tige quickly became obedient. Every boy and girl age twelve and under in town was present, and all carried home a pin with a color picture of Buster Brown on it.

Other companies advertised through free samples. I recall that at the close of one school day, a representative of the Post Cereal Corporation was waiting at the door and passed out tiny packages of Grape Nuts. A year or two later, we were attending the Palo Pinto County Fair at Mineral Wells, and a girl in one of the booths handed me a small bottle of White Karo Syrup. That was the best stuff I ever tasted, and for years I preferred Karo to all other syrups.

Local hardware stores offered a great variety of merchandise. Coal and wood heaters and cooking ranges were sold, but after 1917, Thurber Hardware introduced gas-fired heaters, ranges, and water heaters. All stores displayed hand-powered carpenter's and machinist's tools, coal scuttles, kerosene cans, and large gray cans filled with carbide. Carbide gas fueled miners' lamps and lighted the headlights on early cars. Men purchased guns and ammunition in the hardware stores, and farmers could pick up barbed wire and bundles of baling wire. Saddles, horse and saddle blankets, harness, buggy and bull whips, currycombs and brushes were standard items. Coils of rope encased in burlap sat in a neat row in front of a counter. Loitering customers found them comfortable stools. The stores kept buggies, rigs, surreys, and wagons parked in nearby vacant lots.

For a time there were two hardware stores in Mingus, but the larger of the two, Loflin's Mercantile, burned one night, creating the most spectacular fire in Mingus history. I stood watching the flames, entranced with the pyrotechnic display created by ammunition and other explosives. The building was replaced, but Bob Loflin turned it into a garage. Later he ran an automobile dealership there and operated an office for his Magnolia Petroleum Company agency. The other store, Harwood's Hardware, closed in the mid-1920s, and the Thurber store in the 1930s.

Mingus never had a cemetery, undertaker, hearse, or a dealer in coffins or caskets. One or two cemeteries were located on neighboring farms, but these were private burial grounds. When the Death Angel called, the hearse and coffin came from Gordon, Thurber, or Strawn. In some instances, a family hired a delivery hack or used a farm wagon as the hearse. Most of the Mingus dead were buried in one of the two Gordon cemeteries, a few were interred at Strawn, and some were conveyed to graveyards in adjacent counties. I never knew of a Mingus resident being placed in the company cemetery in Thurber. Friends and neighbors dug the graves in a show of respect for the deceased. Floral offerings were simple, generally being cuttings from rosebushes or flower beds of friends and relatives.

The coffin containing the corpse was kept in the living room (parlor) of the home until it was taken to a local church for the funeral service. I have a faint memory of my baby sister Tempie in her coffin,* which rested on two dining room chairs in the parlor. This was in 1907. Neighbors took turns sitting with the corpse through the night. They also brought mountains of food for family and relatives, washed dishes, and did other household chores until after the funeral. In those days the entire community attended church services and formed the funeral procession to the cemetery.

Only Thurber had a furniture store. People in Mingus went to Thurber, Gordon, or Strawn, or ordered items from a Montgomery Ward catalog. The furniture seen at Thurber was made of wood, with most of it solid oak and maple. The inventory included kitchen tables and cabinets, some covered with metal; chairs and rockers with caned backs and bottoms; and the popular wicker furniture. A variety of wood and iron bedsteads were for sale.

One could also buy a folding bed. This space-saver had a substantial frame with six or eight heavy iron weights under the head to keep it in an upright position when folded up. My parents slept on a bed that folded twice into a dark oak cabinet. As we all four slept in the same bedroom, these beds gave much more room during the day. As our house had no closets, we stored clothing in chiffoniers, chests of drawers, dressers, and chests. In many ways, we lived in a small, cramped world.

Both towns had a number of service shops and other types of businesses, some of which were unique for their time. As a rule we found the local stores quite adequate to our pleasures and needs.

---

*M. Tempie Spratt (July 21, 1906–October 26, 1907), Old Gordon Cemetery, Gordon, Texas.—Ed.

8. Specialty Enterprises

I CAN recall a wizened old man with a very dark complexion and whose face and arms always appeared greasy. He was a Mr. Guy, who operated a butcher shop in Mingus. His wife ran a millinery shop on the first floor of their tiny two-storied house and specialized in trimming, restyling, and fashioning women's hats. Mr. Guy would purchase a steer and butcher it for his market, charging ten and fifteen cents per pound for average cuts of meat and twenty-five cents for choice cuts. But most local families still depended on homemade salt pork and smoked pork and sales were slow. The cost of the ice to keep a carcass fresh ate up most of his profits. Mrs. Guy did little better with her hat business. Local women either bought a hat frame from Mrs. Guy and fashioned their own hats, or they tore up their old hats and created new ones around the old frame. Unable to gain a modest income, the Guys closed their shops before 1910 and moved to Corpus Christi. Their experience was typical of those who operated specialty enterprises in Mingus in the early days.

The specialty business in Mingus included an array of occupations. Not long after the Guys left Mingus, the millinery shop either burned or was torn down and a livery stable and wagonyard was put in there. The livery stable lasted only three or four years. The automobile was creeping into town, and Bob Loflin opened a garage on the site of his old mercantile store. His venture was safe, for it would be some time before the local auto business would justify two garages. Car owners learned to service the simple engines, repair flat tires, change spark plugs and oil, and add water to carbide tanks. The owner of the livery stable razed his building and sold its lumber and sheet iron roofing.

Within a year or two, a restaurant was built on the old Guy lot, and boasted the largest and best lunch counter in Mingus. Lew Jester, an experienced cafe man, operated the place. But the strikes at the coal mines in the early 1920s greatly reduced his trade, and Lew closed out and went to Big Spring, where business was better.

Several restaurants flourished near the railroad tracks. The earliest eating place I recall was in a two-story frame building next to the right-of-way. Reportedly constructed by the T&P, it had a dining room, lunch counter, an upstairs hotel, and a wing with a saloon. It burned and was never rebuilt. Just east of this site was a combination residence and diner, which outlasted them all. It served family style meals to train passengers and was always a family concern. For several years, the Deatons and their girls ran the business, until death took the oldsters, then another family with both boys and girls took over. This ended when the proprietor and his two boys one night walked over to the old Wells Cafe and invited Renzor Bostick, the proprietor, to come outside. Knowing they were coming to give him a good beating, Bostick came out with a six-shooter and killed his would-be assailant. Even though the grand jury no-billed him for the killing, Renzor moved his family to Fort Worth. The Minyard family then came in and operated the old man's cafe until the T&P phased out its local business.

In the meantime, cafe owner Herbert Wells had concluded that he could do better as a house painter, as there was no painter in town. He became a good one. Dad's home stayed white for twenty or thirty years after Herb painted it. After completing a round of painting in Mingus and Strawn, Herb found himself out of work and moved to Oklahoma City.

When three or four lunchrooms were operating in Mingus, each manager would send an employee out with a brass handbell, large gong, or huge triangle when a train stopped for lunch. As passengers stepped off the coaches, each cafe representative clanged or banged with great fury, hoping to draw hungry customers to his eating place. The din they created was unbelievable.

Mingus had only one tin shop when I was a kid, and it played a major role in the well-being of the town. In contrast to Thurber, whose residents had access to running water and ice, Mingusites had no water faucets and used ice sparsely. Every resident and business-man relied on a dug cistern, a metal cistern, or on Old Man Roark's water wagon. The railroad was the exception, hauling in its water supply in special cars. The tinsmith provided vital services to water users. He was an expert at fabricating metal tanks. A customer could hand him the dimensions of the tank desired and indicate the num-ber of faucets. The smith used snips to cut sheets of galvanized metal, made rivet holes with a metal punch, and hand-bradded the rivets.

Brushing acid along the metal edges to be soldered, he reached for soldering irons heated white hot on a small charcoal furnace, melted solder along the seams, and sealed the tank. The tinsmith also made gutter pipes and troughs, soldering them together and fastening them under house eaves, with drainpipes running down to the cistern. I enjoyed watching this craftsman at work and was amazed how smoothly he spread solder into perfect joints.

Cisterns and gutters were not the only items the tinsmith made. He carefully fitted zinc sheets over kitchen tables and specialized in building milk coolers. These coolers or troughs were made of wood and lined with a zinc sheeting and had a drain spout in the bottom. Our cooler was about six feet long, a foot wide and six inches deep, and sat in a frame four feet high. We filled the trough half full of water and placed pails and gallon crocks of milk in the water, wrapping each container with cloths. The trough occupied a shady nook with ventilation, and the cloths, dampened by capillary action, kept milk and butter fairly cool. In the summer, sweet milk soured in about twenty-four hours, but that was no loss. We poured the soured milk into the butter churn, allowed it to clabber, then sweetened the clabber and ate it as a dessert or made it into cottage cheese.

Many housewives had been reared to use springs of water or deep wells for cooling, but we had neither in Mingus. Milk troughs were the next best thing. Money was scarce and ice was considered expensive at forty cents per hundred pounds. Even when an icebox showed up to pay a doctor bill, Mother continued to use her old milk trough to keep costs down.

Although the tinsmith could fashion large metal troughs to hold stock water, we never had use of these around the place. Dad picked up a heavy wooden trough about twenty feet long when the brewery closed down. It held about a hundred gallons of water and was filled at regular intervals from Roark's water wagon.

After 1915 a building slump hit Mingus, and the tinsmith faced hard times. A few brick stores replaced frame structures that burned, but residential construction was at a standstill. This depressed the demand for gutters and metal cisterns. People also found they could purchase these items from mail order houses. Refrigerators drove milk troughs from homes. Basically, a change in technology spelled doom for the tin shop.

The woodshop and lumberyard in Mingus soon went the way of the tin shop. Unlike the situation in Thurber, where the T&P ordered lumber and shingles by carload directly from the mills, the Mingus lumberyard depended primarily on local business. When frame construction dwindled, the yard closed down and the building was razed and hauled away.

The woodworking tools in the cabinet shop always fascinated me. Almost without exception they were hand tools. There was a saw for every purpose: fine tooth for cutting boards; coarse tooth for ripping; keyhole saws for cutting arcs or circles; and hacksaws. The combination plane had gadgets that guided the cutting edge in a straight line to cut a groove. The plane had blades with cutting edges of every conceivable shape and width. A novice gazing at the multitude of different tools in the chests of these wood craftsmen stood in awe. Chests, tables, yard and porch swings, as well as benches and chairs, composed much of the shopwork. The inventory of lumber consisted mostly of white and yellow pine, along with small amounts of hardwoods.

The Thurber print shop was in operation before Dad came to Mingus. A property of the Texas & Pacific Mercantile and Manufacturing Company, it published the *Thurber Journal* every Saturday. The paper was delivered free to town residents, but nonresidents paid one dollar a year for a subscription. The company used a large amount of stationery and required a variety and quantity of paper for its many and diverse enterprises. The *Journal*, in the absence of radio, or even telephones, was an inexpensive medium for communicating with the public. It featured a two-column billing of Opera House shows for the coming week, ads for the dry goods and hardware stores (and for the Overland motor car when the company became a dealer), plus an occasional ad from the outside. For example, in 1917, the Texas & Pacific Railway ran a double-column advertisement announcing daily excursion rates to Mineral Wells, Texas. At that time Mineral Wells was the spa of Central West Texas.

Around 1910 Mingus briefly boasted a job printshop, which published the *Mingus Herald*, a weekly. I think Bond was the name of the owner-editor, and he must have been one of the most courageous men in the world. His press, frames of type, stock, and shop equipment would not have covered half the bed of John Dyer's dray. Bond ran his press in an unpainted frame building with a ten-by-twenty-foot floor space. Job printing was practically nonexistent. Dad had Bond print five hundred professional cards that read "J. T. Spratt, M.D., Internal Medicine, Diseases of Women and Children a Specialty, Mingus, Texas, Office Phone 18, Residence Phone 24." That batch of cards lasted him a lifetime. Bond had to contend with Jim Son's *Palo Pinto County Star*, at the county seat, which controlled the printing business locally. Also, few people in Mingus subscribed to daily newspapers, and the handful of merchants did little advertising. The town was never known for its prolific readers.

The *Mingus Herald* was a one-man operation. Throughout the day, passersby could see Bond at the typecases, galley stick in hand, setting type letter by letter with the speed of a none-too-hungry rooster picking grains of corn from the ground. Toward the end of the week, he had moved from typesetting to the press, and cranked out the weekly issue, one copy at a time. Bond stayed around only a few months, then loaded his printing equipment in a wagon and moved on.

The unpainted shack that housed the *Herald* saw many short-lived ventures. Its monthly rent of five dollars was its principal attractive feature. On one occasion, an old, worn-out lawyer set up an office there and hung around for several months. A criminal attorney could find work, but there was no call for a civil lawyer. And those needing a criminal lawyer hired one who had an established practice in Palo Pinto or Erath counties.

The old shanty also housed a bakeshop. We bought cinnamon rolls there that were the best I ever ate. They were pinwheels of dough rolled thin and coated with cinnamon, then rolled up, sliced into one-inch wheels, and baked. The baker spread a white icing over each batch. Rolls from the Mingus bakery were short on dough but long on icing and cinnamon.

We never needed a cobbler's shop in Mingus, for every family did its own shoe repair. A home kit contained a hammer, a half-dozen shoe lasts, ranging in size from the toddler's foot to that of an adult, and a knife for cutting and trimming leather. The kit also had an awl for punching holes in the leather, a cake of beeswax, and a heavy needle for stitching and mending shoes or broken harness. Three or four boxes of brass cobbler nails of various lengths, along with "shoe blacking" and a brush, completed the kit. Boys became proficient at an early age at half-soling shoes, fastening soles to inner soles with nails. The main trick, after trimming the sole to fit the shoe, was to make sure you had the metal last directly under the nail being driven. This ensured a well-bradded nail point. Taking off for school or a party wearing shoes where a nail had not been bradded correctly guaranteed the early return home of a hobbling cripple.

Since Mingus was a railroad division point with a half dozen switch engine crews, a watchmaker should have found regular business in town. About 1912 a German watchmaker by the name of Schneider built a combination shop and living quarters adjacent to Joe Abraham's store. As he had no electricity, he installed a large glass window across the shop front to ensure adequate light for his delicate work. He had no family, but did own a beautiful black horse, which he rode back and forth to Thurber and other neighboring towns to collect and deliver clocks and watches needing repair. Like other livestock owners in Mingus, Schneider grazed his horse on vacant lots and along street fence rows. He had an unusual method of making the horse come to him. He would walk down the street, call and whistle, and when this failed, he threw cinders or pebbles at the animal. When he registered a hit, the horse came trotting to him.

Schneider was a good repairman, but he did not last long. World War I started a year or two after he opened his shop, and when this country entered the conflict, it was rumored that Schneider was a German spy. Passing his shop one day, I noticed him working on a watch and stopped and glued my nose to the plate glass to get a better view of his work. After a time, he asked me what I was doing. "I'm just watching," was my reply, to which he retorted, "Do I need watching?" That worried me later when I began to hear the spy rumor. I wondered why a German spy would be in Mingus, unless to blow up a T&P railroad bridge or two, or to try to organize German farmers north of town and the few Germans working in Thurber. The rumor grew and threats followed. Finally Schneider closed his shop and left town. As far as I know, no Germans in the area were molested.

Joe Teichman, a German who raised wheat on Dodson Prairie northeast of town, ran a flour mill in Mingus. A number of German families had settled on the prairie before the turn of the century, and most of them prospered. They grew grains, especially wheat, and livestock. About 1915 Teichman built a small flour mill in town. I watched every phase of the construction and operation. I was particularly fascinated by the silk screens that sifted the flour from the bran, after the grain had been crushed by a series of rollers. A large gasoline engine furnished the power, and only two men were needed to run the mill. Joe stored flour in one set of bins and bran in another and filled sacks from each bin between mill runs. The sacks were plain and unattractive, featuring only a simple brand name and Mingus Flour Mill printed in black or blue ink.

In building his flour mill, Teichman ran counter to the trend. For half a century, the movement toward combination or consolidation had been in full swing, and milling was done principally by large companies with distinctive sacks bearing widely known brand names and symbols. In addition, housewives preferred bleached flour that baked into cakes and biscuits of untinted whiteness. Unfortunately, Teichman's screen at his Mingus mill could not sift out the golden hue that characterized unbleached flour. Joe sold flour for twelve or more years, but never prospered. Mother was a bleached flour woman and was devoted to the American Beauty brand. As long as we kept a milk cow around the place, we fed the animal bran from Teichman's mill. But he could never break the brand-name barrier and finally closed his operations. The building was torn down and the equipment sold.

Hankins ran a blacksmith's shop in a weather-beaten, barnlike structure with a dirt floor carpeted with cinders. Against one wall a stack of worn-out horseshoes stood ten or twelve feet high and measured eight feet in diameter at the base. They were the discards from shoeing horses. Henry Wadsworth Longfellow may have placed his smithy under a spreading chestnut, but he failed miserably in depicting the marvelous things a blacksmith could do with a piece of iron. When Hankins was not using his forge, he had a large stick jammed down in its coals. There was always an ember on the end of the stick, and with a few pumps of the bellows he had the coal in the forge ablaze in a few seconds. Like all good blacksmiths, Hankins was an artist. Holding a red hot shoe on an anvil, he gave it only a few taps to make it fit the hoof to be shod. To cool and harden the shoe he doused it in a half-sized barrel of water sitting nearby.

Hankins did more than shoe horses. He had a metal trough with the bottom arched to fit the curvature of wagon or buggy wheels. He kept this trough filled with a light oil and used it to cool and shrink a metal tire, which had been heated and placed around a wheel. This was a common practice for tightening a loose tire. Hankins also made iron pokers for heaters, fireplaces, or steam tractors, and shovels for cleaning ashes or cinders from stoves or fireplaces. He repaired plows and sharpened plow points. However, his real bread-and-butter income came from shoeing horses and mules.

Although the appearance of the automobile closed the livery stable, it did not drive Hankins out of business. Gasoline-powered tractors crept into the Southwest much more slowly than in the Midwest. Thus horses and mules remained the basic sources of power on many farms after the families had traded their buggies and surrey for Fords. This kept Hankins and other blacksmiths in business for a time, but their days were numbered. Well before 1920, Hankins was gone and so was his blacksmithing.

Bill Rigsby is the only person I recall who operated, or managed, the same type of business in both Mingus and Thurber. He ran a small cotton gin in Mingus for a year or two, but quickly found that the amount of cotton grown locally was insufficient to make his business profitable. After 1910 Bill loaded his machinery in a farm wagon, hitched up to the steam tractor that powered the gin, and moved to Morgan Mill in Erath County. He ran the gin there for several years before disposing of it. Some time in the early 1920s the T&P Company erected a gin in Thurber, which was among the last of their small undertakings, and hired Bill Rigsby to operate it; however, almost from the beginning, its days were numbered, too.

There was no parade of short-lived enterprises in Thurber as there was in Mingus. The fundamental reason for the difference was that every shop or store in Mingus, with few exceptions, was an individual proprietorship or a partnership. This meant that the cafe, tin shop, saloon, picture show, blacksmith shop, and other kinds of stores had to show a profit. Each enterprise had to succeed or perish. In Thurber, the Texas & Pacific Mercantile and Manufacturing Company owned all the enterprises. Each store carried a distinct identification: the Market Department, the Grocery Department, the Dry Goods Department, and the Hardware Department. Other departments included the Drug Store, the Saloon, the Picture Show, and the Opera House, along with the *Thurber Journal.*

Even though the T&P Company ran a variety of businesses, the consolidated statement of profits and losses was the important thing. In some instances, a department may not have shown an annual profit, but the T&P still kept it in operation. For example, the *Thurber Journal* probably made little money, but it saved the company substantial amounts on its printing bills—which could be considered profits. Also, the free circulation of the paper influenced profits, and the company saw it as a valuable means to communicate with its employees and keep marketable items of the several departments before the public. The *Mingus Herald* had no options; it either operated at a profit or it closed.

Eventually, the business units in Thurber faced attrition. In 1921, the year before the last strike, company stores reaped substantial profits, but the year following, their losses were awesome. However, the company was not in trouble. It had changed its name to the Texas & Pacific Coal and Oil Company and quickly became a highly profitable organization. It could have operated its Thurber stores at a loss for at least a dozen years, mainly as a convenience for company management and office workers, so long as it showed consolidated profits.

One final comment on specialties. Thurberites had a major advantage over Mingusites when it came to foods. The company's huge cold storage vault with its market assured town residents a choice of fresh fruits and vegetables the year around. Seafoods and fish, both salt and fresh water, were available at the market almost any time. Shoppers from Mingus were welcome to purchase these items, but few of them did. The two miles between the two towns represented quite a barrier. A horse and buggy trip to Thurber, including the time for harnessing and unharnessing the horse, ate up the greater part of two hours. Few jumped in the buggy and ran over to Thurber just to buy a grapefruit or a pint of fresh oysters.

9. Chores

IN THE early 1900s, remnants of the frontier still lingered in Texas. Thurber miners tore coal with pick and shovel from veins deep underground, and burros pulled it to the shaft. Mule-drawn wagons hauled freight from the depot. Farmers used animal power for heavy work on the farm and relied on families and relatives to hoe weeds, chop and pick cotton, and gather, shuck, and shell corn. Housewives labored long hours each day at cooking and other household chores. These tasks were hard, and men and women became stoop-shouldered at an early age. Working people were middle-aged at thirty, and many looked like old crones at fifty. I lived in this period of transition from the frontier and experienced some of the chores that kids had known for hundreds of years.

Our day began shortly after dawn. Everyone was up and busy. While Mother prepared breakfast, Dad climbed into the hayloft and tossed down blocks of Johnson grass hay for the horse and cow, then poured a gallon of oats or a dozen ears of shucked corn in the feed bin for the horse. He then carried a bundle of hay to the cow lot and threw it in the feed rack. A gallon and a half of bran, dampened to protect the animal against the heaves, supplemented the hay. Then he did the milking, always taking care to strip the cow (drain the last drop of milk from her udder) to keep her from going dry. After taking the pails of milk to the house, Dad slopped the hogs and gave them a dozen or so ears from the corncrib. Eventually all of these chores fell to me.

By the time Dad had finished tending the livestock, Mother had two dozen biscuits in the oven. Baking biscuits was a ritual. Every morning she opened the flour bin, took out a large bread pan, a rolling pin, a tin can with one end cut out to serve as a biscuit cutter, and a flour sifter. She emptied any leftover flour, plus fresh flour, into the sifter, and created a perfect cone. Bunching the fingers of her right hand, she jabbed them into the cone with a twisting motion, and into this crater dumped a cup of buttermilk and a handful of lard. Next came a pinch of salt, a teaspoonful of baking powder (KC always made the biscuits rise), and a touch of soda (Arm & Hammer, of course). Mother slowly kneaded the flour, lard, and buttermilk into dough, dropped the dough onto a rolling board, which had been sprinkled with flour to prevent sticking, and rolled it to a half-inch thickness. She then cut it into circles and popped them into the oven. When they came from the oven, the biscuits were always golden brown with white, fluffy insides.

While the biscuits were baking, Mother fixed the breakfast trimmings. She fried bacon, sausage, or ham, then used the grease for gravy—cream gravy, if bacon were fried, or red-eye gravy, if sausage or ham were the meat. Eggs—fried, scrambled, or soft-boiled—rounded out the main meal. With buttered biscuits (home-churned butter) went molasses or preserves. During school months, fried chicken often replaced the pork products. Flapjacks could show up any morning during the summer, but only on weekends or for the evening meal during the rest of the year.

Not all the twenty-four biscuits were consumed at breakfast. One or two showed up in our school lunch with chicken, ham, or sausage. Another was usually buttered and filled with thick preserves. There also might be a small jar of frijoles from the day before, a sour pickle, or an onion, green or fresh, depending on the season. An occasional apple or a pear gave variety to our lunch. The biscuits reappeared at the evening meal, and the dogs got the scraps, sopped in the left-over gravy, plus any meat. If biscuits accumulated over several days, Mother added sweet milk, sugar, raisins, and cinnamon and made a cold bread pudding. After a biscuit had been baked in our household, it was never thrown away.

As soon as he got up from the table, Dad put the old strop and straight razor to work. In keeping with his professional dignity, he shaved every day. There was a barbershop near the railroad with a row of shaving mugs for regular customers, but he went there only for haircuts. The men around Mingus and Thurber usually shaved once a week, and trimmed their hair every month or two. Dad used a set of barber clippers on Harry and me, almost scalping us each time. I was in high school before a barber cut my hair, even though haircuts were only a quarter. While Dad was shaving, Mother straightened the bedding so we could raise their big fold-down bed to its upright position and give our bed its double-folding.

Each school day, Harry and I combed our hair, washed our face and hands, put on a clean shirt, and got a fresh handkerchief. Nearly all the kids carried their lunches in paper sacks, but we had to lug ours in a lunch basket or a dinner pail, and we hated it. School "took up books" at 8:oo.

Shortly after mid-morning recess one day, some youngster filched a biscuit sandwich (filled with butter and preserves) from a neighbor's lunch basket, checked to see that teacher's back was turned, then kicked the biscuit across the aisle. The culprit then opened his geography book and ducked behind it, shielding a devilish grin from the prying eyes of the teacher. Every desk top quickly became the repository for an open geography and the poor biscuit began its travels from front to rear and side to side on the classroom floor. The teacher was aware something peculiar was taking place, but never detected what. I don't remember the name of a single kid in the room, nor, for that matter, who the teacher was, but in later years, my memory would often haul out the biscuit from the old lunch pail and relive that singular event.

Another vivid memory of my school days concerns the first year that Bob Moreland was our school principal.* Some of the boys were tough and Moreland knew this. At noon one day, the new principal was seen on campus with a cut of tobacco in his mouth. This was something; now everybody could smoke. For three days the boys' outhouse took on the essence of a smokehouse filled with fresh pork and fired with all the green chips in the county. Then Moreland sent word for the boys to meet him in the auditorium. When they had assembled, he took out his plug of tobacco and spoke to them as follows: "Boys, I have been chewing tobacco at noon for the past three days. I did it to show you that I like my tobacco as well as any man. But school is no place to chew, smoke, or dip. Here is my plug. Any of you can examine it at the end of the day to see whether it's been touched. The remainder of the school year, none of us will use tobacco—to, from, or during school hours. This applies also to the outhouse."

Some of the rougher group had to try out Moreland to see if he could run the show. They found out that he could apply his belt with vigor to the seat of a pair of pants on a boy bent over a desk. Moreland never exacted punishment the instant that guilt was established. He dismissed the guilty with, "Well, boys, we'll wait a few days for the tanning, wait until we are all in a good humor." When he introduced this waiting period, there was a good bit of speculation. Would there

---

*Parts of the Moreland story appeared in John S. Spratt, "When Bob Threw Christmas Away," *Southwest Review* 53 (Winter 1968): 86–87. Used with the permission of the Southern Methodist University Press.—Ed.

really be any tanning? There was. After a few days, sometimes a week, the principal would appear at the classroom door and beckon to a boy, who shortly returned taking his seat in a gingerly manner. Those waiting periods were more painful than the strapping.

One hoped that Moreland might forget, but his elephantine memory never failed. The ones receiving the belt passed the word. He could lay it on, but never stopped smiling and always shook hands with the culprit while telling him he hoped this to be the last time they would meet under such circumstances. It worked. The roughest and toughest knew they had a schoolmaster who could be neither bluffed nor run over.

Bob Moreland roomed with the Rosseau family, who lived in a four-room box house with the kitchen in a shed room at the rear. The house had been built by a former railroad employee who had toted, piece by piece, most of the lumber from the railroad carshops. Lumber for a number of houses in the community had come from the shops in the same manner. None came as a gift from the company, nor was it stolen. It was either scrap lumber, or the railroad owned it. The Rosseaus assigned the front bedroom to the principal.

Moreland's room was about ten by ten by nine. Its furnishings included a bed, washstand with pitcher and basin, chiffonier, small coal heater, and a lonely Currier and Ives print hanging on the wall in a gilded frame. The walls were covered with a faded floral paper. Green shades hung over the windows, but there were no drapes or curtains. An ornate kerosene lamp sat on a bedside table. As the room was confining, Bob Moreland used it only for sleeping quarters.

After school the redheaded schoolman usually walked down to the post office. He was quite a talker, so, after picking up his mail, he would join the spit and whittle club on the sidewalk in front of the bank, or make his way to the South Side Drug Store owned by the Rosseaus. There, seated at one of the tables, he would toy with a lemon soda or a glass of Hires Root Beer and while away an hour or so until suppertime. A pleasant, smiling man, Bob Moreland was long remembered in our little West Texas community.

When Dad left for his office or to make morning calls, Mother turned to household chores. She might spend several hours crocheting, darning socks, or patching clothes. Or she would join the women at the Baptist church for an all-day quilting session. This group donated to charity the quilt tops, linings, and cotton paddings they made. The quilts usually went to Buckner's Orphan Home in Dallas.

Like other housewives of that day, Mother did the family ironing—and everything had to be ironed. This included bed sheets, pillowcases, underwear, dresses, shirts, overalls, petticoats, tablecloths, and dresser scarves. Cup towels and face towels were about the only things that escaped the iron. Mother heated two or three flatirons on the kitchen range or set them up facing a burning fireplace. When one cooled and would not smooth out wrinkles, it was exchanged for one on the stove. Ironing boards resting on the top of kitchen chairbacks saved the ironer many steps. Mother kept a pad of beeswax on the ironing board and frequently ran a hot iron across the pad to ensure a smooth ironing surface.

Mother prepared a snack for Dad at noon, then returned to her chores. In spring she had hens to set and baby chicks to tend. She fiddled around with rosebushes, and for about nine months out of the year worked in our vegetable garden. There were vegetables to be gathered, cleaned, and cooked for supper. For an active person, there was no end to the things that a housewife did about the house each day.

When school "let out books" at 4:00, some four hundred kids headed for home. Three or four came to school by buggy, one or two rode horseback, but all the others walked. This was the time for boys to have fistfights to settle disputes that had arisen through the day, or you could walk your best girl home while carrying her books. After school also was the safest time to smoke a cigarette or chew tobacco, both of which were forbidden by parents and school rules. Boys and girls played hooky whenever possible, but Dad constantly moved about on his rounds and I was sure he would catch me if I tried it. Or some busybody would inform him that he had seen me with a group of boys headed for the creek during the middle of the afternoon.

When I got home, there was a multitude of chores waiting. We were one of the few families in Mingus who burned wood; practically everybody else burned Thurber coal. As a result, in the early fall Harry and I sawed wood for range and heater. The sawing went on day after day for weeks. Our heater and range had large maws and seemed to consume boatloads of wood. Each afternoon we filled one or two woodboxes and carried out ashes from the stoves by the bucketful.

One hot September afternoon, Harry and I had the crosscut saw going, and every few minutes we would stop and get a drink of water. Our parents were off somewhere and would not be back until late afternoon. I remembered that a bottle of Mother's toddy whiskey was in the house and decided to make a drink. I filled an empty baking pail, which held about a quart, almost full of water and finished it off with whiskey and sugar. It really tasted good—so good in fact that during the afternoon I returned to the pail about every fifteen minutes. The pail was soon empty. That evening I got through supper all right, but in trying to do my homework, I could not stay awake. When I got up and prepared for bed, Dad and Mother wanted to know what was wrong. "Nothing. Just sleepy," I replied. That did not pass as a satisfactory answer, so the quizzing continued and my brother, Harry, finally spilled the beans. I was permitted to go to bed, but only after a stern lecture that henceforth I would not drink whiskey raw or mixed with drinking water.

Every evening we halted the wood sawing to gather eggs, feed the animals and poultry, and milk the cow. The night meal was a fair repeat of the morning fare, except there might be supplements of frijoles, hominy, fried potatoes, and cake or pie for dessert. Harry and I did the dishes after each evening meal during school months, and for all three meals on the weekends and during the summer. In addition, on Saturdays we cleaned the house and mopped floors. And for years on Saturday my assignment also included baking the Sunday cake.

By the time we had sawed and neatly ricked the stovewood for winter, another annual task appeared. The hogs were fat and cold weather was not far off. When the first Texas blue norther came roaring in, I hated to see the school day end. I knew what I would find when I got home—unless Dad was tied up with an O.B. case. He would have the old wash pot filled with boiling water, the butcher knives sharpened, the single-shot 22 rifle loaded and lying on the wash bench, a singletree suspended from the shed roof by a heavy wire, and his work clothes on.

Dad would kill one of the hogs with the rifle, and he and I would drag the carcass from the sty to a metal barrel filled with boiling water and propped up at a thirty-degree tilt. As we eased first one end of the hog and then the other into the barrel to scald it, Mother added more boiling water and stoked the fire. When the hog was thoroughly scalded, we dragged it onto several loose boards, picked up the knives and began scraping off the hair, turning the carcass from side to side as we worked.

After the animal had been thoroughly shaved, we thrust a singletree under the leaders of the hind legs and pulled the carcass up by block and tackle so that it swung in the air. With a sharp butcher knife, Dad slit the carcass down the middle of the belly and bisected the rib cage. He quickly removed the insides, discarding everything but the heart and liver. A strip of tenderloin was then ripped from the sides of the backbone. Here I would begin my hopeless plea to have some of it fried for supper. The answer was always no. It had to be ground and mixed into sausage to preserve the proper lean-fat balance. It never made sense to see the choicest part of the hog lose its savor in a batch of lard. With a sharp ax, Dad chopped the bones from either side of the backbone and tore out the rib cage.

We ate spareribs and backbone while still fresh. Mother cooked the backbone by stewing, and either stewed or fried the ribs. Whatever was stewed, there would be corn dumplings. These were simple patties formed by pouring boiling water over the meal and then patting out cakes and stewing them with the ribs or backbone. They were delicious but greasy. Mother sandwiched liver fried with onions in between meals of spareribs or backbone. I hated the stuff as a kid.

Grandma Felts, who lived across the street, always took the feet, head, and heart. She pickled the feet for Grandpa, who was as fond of them as he was of baked opossum. The ears went into hogshead sauce. Grandpa liked the brains scrambled with eggs. With the remainder of the head, Grandma made hogshead pudding. She boiled the head until the lean flesh could be removed, mixed it with cornmeal, and cooked it to the texture of a thick pudding. This was poured into pans to cool, and it would keep for several weeks. Sliced, battered in flour, and fried to a golden brown, the pudding was equal in flavor to the tenderloin.

Dad finished the butchering process by carefully trimming the shoulders, sides, and hams for sausage. The fat trimmings went into one dishpan, and the lean went into another. As the pans were filled, we carried them to the kitchen. Mother had a hot fire going in the range in readiness for rendering lard from the fat. She would begin by cutting the leaner trimmings for the sausage mill, which had been securely fastened to a corner of the kitchen table. Cranking pork through the mill would go on for hours and hours. A quantity of sage and perhaps one or two other ingredients were worked into the freshly ground pork.

With everything thoroughly mixed, she fashioned sausage patties and dumped them in large skillets of piping hot, freshly rendered lard. When cooked, the patties then went into gallon syrup pails, layer upon layer; melted lard was poured over them and a lid carefully sealed the pail. This process was repeated over and over until all the fatty trimming had been rendered into lard, and every speck of lean had been ground for sausage. There was always a surplus of lard rendered, and this went into separate tin pails, which were sealed and stored in the cellar. The sausage was dug out through the year and heated for meals, and buckets of lard were reclaimed for cooking purposes.

We carried the pork sides and hams to a large salt bin in the smokehouse. The bin could hold several hundred pounds of pork. Every piece of fresh pork was buried in several sacks of salt to keep flies from penetrating the meat. For some reason, Dad never smoke-cured his pork. We never drew any pork from the salt bath until the liver, spareribs, and backbone had been consumed. Mother fried some of the sides as bacon, but it was used mostly for seasoning in cooking vegetables, fresh or fried. Through the winter and spring, salted hams and shoulders were fairly palatable, but as the hot summer wore on every ham we cut into was greener than the one before. It still puzzles me why we did not all die from pork poisoning. We annually replenished the pork supply by at least two more butcherings each winter.

After hog killing, we had other delicacies. Each time we butchered, Grandpa Felts claimed the pigtails as they were severed from the backbone. He relished them over any desserts, especially if they were stewed and well-seasoned. After lard had been rendered and poured off, Mother carefully preserved the cracklings. A few of them, while fresh, went into crackling bread. The older folks relished it, but I never found it appetizing. We poured most of the cracklings into flour sacks and kept them in the cellar for soap making.

When Mother had sufficient cracklings and other fatty orts, she ordered the soapmaking crew into action. We carefully weighed the cracklings and fat scraps, so many pounds to one can of Giant Lye, then filled the washpot with water and built a fire under it. When the water began to boil, Mother dropped in a can of lye and stirred it with a long-handled paddle until the lye had dissolved. We then pitched the cracklings and odds and ends of fat into the boiling lye water. Then came my job, to stir and stir with a long-handled paddle, more accurately an oar, which had been fashioned by trimming a one-by-six, six feet long. When the lye dissolved the cracklings, we extinguished the fire, but kept up the stirring until the soap thickened. We then covered the pot to keep out floating coal cinders and allowed it to cool. By the next morning the new batch of lye soap was solid enough to be sliced into cakes and placed on the wash bench for further drying before use.

This soap, a color between a tan and a light brown, was primarily used for washing laundry and dishes and not for hands and faces or bathing. As red, rough, lye-soap hands were quite common, Dad concocted a mixture, mostly of glycerine, which he called Spratt's Cosmetic, which gave a measure of relief to chapped hands. He sold large quantities of it through the years.

Our old black pot had other uses. On washdays we filled it with water, built a fire, and pitched in large chunks of lye soap. When the water began to boil, Mother dropped in a batch of white clothes and punched them with an old broom stick for ten or fifteen minutes, before lifting them out with the stick and carrying them to a wash-tub. The colored things came next. While they boiled, the white clothes received further treatment with lye soap on the rub board, then went to a tub of blued rinsing water. Scarves, pillowcases, petticoats, Dad's dress shirts, and Mother's drawers went from the rinse water to a pan of starch. Before hanging out clothes, we thoroughly wiped the clotheslines with a wet cloth to remove all the soot. By 1920 we ended hog butchering and substituted Castile for lye soap.

Three or four families had mechanical washing machines in Mingus. Aunt Rosa Felts owned one, which she operated by turning a crank geared to a rotor that resembled a four-legged milk stool. The four legs jerked the clothing about 180 degrees in each direction. The machine also had an old-fashioned clothes wringer. An even more ancient washer was operated by jerking a vertical handle back and forth. It had a tub built in the shape of a 180-degree arc, and inside was a cradle curved to conform to the tub. Rounded-edged slats made the bottom of the cradle. A lever tumbled the clothing back and forth. These machines eliminated the rub board, but turning a crank or jerking a lever back and forth was equally tiring. Mother bought her first electric iron about 1915, but she never owned a washing machine.

Several families sent clothing to steam laundries in Weatherford or Fort Worth. Laundry shipped by passenger train once a week from Mingus returned three or four days later. It was shipped in heavy canvas baskets built around a metal frame with wooden bottoms and lids. The lids could be locked for shipment and rollers were attached to the bottoms. Most of the laundry bundles consisted of men's dress shirts and detachable white stiff collars. Men often sent only collars, asking their wives to launder their shirts. Some shirts also sported stiff detachable cuffs. These also made frequent trips back and forth from Weatherford in laundry baskets.

Although a Chinese had operated the railroad restaurant and hotel in Mingus that burned, we never had a Chinese laundry, nor do I recall one in Thurber. Earl Brown ran a cleaning and pressing shop, as well as a tailor shop, for a number of years. But he always sent customers' measurements into Fort Worth or Dallas for the tailoring, receiving commissions for these orders. Shortly after the railroad and mine strikes in 1921, he closed his shop and moved to Brownwood. By this time, a dry cleaning firm in Stephenville began weekly pick-up and delivery service in Mingus. As a high school student in Weatherford (1918–1920), I took all of my shirts and collars to the lone Chinese laundryman in town there.

Occasionally, I was involved in farm chores. Uncle Charlie Felts,

Mother's brother, owned a two-hundred-acre farm on the edge of Mingus. He was a fine carpenter and an excellent cabinetmaker, but he plied these trades only during off seasons of farm work. His principal crops were Johnson grass hay, wheat, and oats. As a teenager I worked with him and his boys baling hay, harvesting, and threshing wheat and oats. We always admired the pecan trees that stood along the creek bank and out in the field. Each year Mother would take us to join the Felts family in gathering pecans on the halves. Shelling a few jars for the kitchen was a community project.

Then there was our vegetable garden, which tripled in size as Dad acquired three-fourth's ownership of our block. He hired a man with a span of mules and turning plow to break the garden every four or five years, but otherwise we worked it with a garden fork, rake, hoe, and hand plow. Mother was a confirmed believer in planting everything by the moon, and at certain times before and after Easter. Her guidebook was Wine of Cardui's *Ladies Almanac and Weather Guide*. She also relied heavily on the packet of garden seed mailed each fall or winter by congressmen to their constituents. The packet contained just about everything needed for planting a garden, except tomato plants and onion sets. But Tom Blanton ruined that for her.* He regarded the free seeds as an extravagant expenditure of the taxpayers' money and made the matter his principal issue in his successful race for Congress in 1916. I am not sure what Blanton had to do with it, but soon after he took his seat, the annual packet of free garden seed stopped.

What we did as a family in Mingus was duplicated all over the country. Many even grew their own popcorn, but we never did, because Grandpa Felts raised enough for both families in his garden across the street. Nor did we work around the clock day after day. Only Dad did that—as a physician—and only when an epidemic swept the country or a rash of pneumonia cases appeared during the winter. Most of the things we did were work, but not heavy manual labor. There also were opportunities for games, hunting and fishing trips, and holidays, when we spent days and days preparing mountains of food. But we always considered this more fun than labor.

---

*Thomas L. Blanton (1872–1957) grew up in Houston, graduated from the University of Texas Law School, and was elected to Congress in 1916 (Webb, *Handbook of Texas*, III, 88).—Ed.

10. Life around Home

URING MOST of the year, life around home was fairly routine. A regular cycle of lessons, sports, and reading occupied our time, but in the summer we often visited the Ross Ranch north of Pecos and in the fall there was the hunting season. We looked forward to each, for they were always memorable occasions.

At every evening meal, the family discussed daily happenings. What one had done, what had happened to one, was important to all. But some things were said and never mentioned outside the family circle. This applied especially to the doctor's patients. As a rule he never talked much about his medical practice for ethical reasons. If report cards had been sent home, they became a topic of conversation. My parents carefully scrutinized the grades and the marks for deportment. Some kids received extra money for good cards, but we never did. There was the devil to pay if our class grades were below normal.

We always feared strappings. One late afternoon Dad walked to the back porch, took down his razor strop, and called to Harry and me. His face bore a stern look, as he held the strop in a foreboding manner. "What's this I've been hearing about you two boys?" Telling my brother to stretch out his hand, Dad raised the strop. He probably called on Harry first because he invariably screamed before a blow was struck. This time Harry outdid himself with a wail of agony as the strop descended. But Dad whopped it against the porch wall, and his face broke into a broad grin. He shook hands and complimented us for being good boys, and handed each of us a fifty-cent piece.

I was a little ashamed to take the money. I had smoked two or three forbidden cigarettes the week before while hidden in a deep ditch that ran between the schoolhouse and home. I was certain that someone had seen me and reported the fact to Dad. Anyway, I decided that giving up my clandestine smoking quarters for a period of time might be a wise course of action.

Mother's mealtime conversation focused on her own sphere. We heard how many pounds of butter she had churned and how many she could sell, along with the number of eggs on hand and how many dozen she might market. At other times we learned that the chicks were beginning to hatch. Or that mites or lice were in the henhouse and that she might have to get rid of the chickens before they began to kill them. Sometimes she wondered just when Bill would drop her calf. She had been dry so long that milk and butter for the family were becoming a problem.

As soon as the kitchen had been cleaned in the evening, we studied our lessons. Sometimes we were so tired from chores, we did little more than sit and stare at a book. Spelling was an exception. My parents always gave out the words to be spelled next day. If they had not been thoroughly memorized, more boning was required. I never felt one tiny speck of sympathy for Abe Lincoln. He had a blazing fireplace before which he could stretch out on his belly and read, but I studied by a matchlike flame from a tiny coal oil lamp.

On these evenings, Mother usually turned to her crocheting and embroidering, and Dad would browse through a medical journal or read a newspaper several days old. Once a week he read Jim Son's *Palo Pinto County Star*. On evenings with no school days to follow, we played games. Sets of dominoes and checkers, along with a deck of Bicycle playing cards, always rested on the dining room plate rail. After Dad won the phonograph and records from I. A. Fine's sales promotion scheme, its noise ended all efforts at mental concentration.

Sunday was a special day. Sickness was the only excuse for not being at Sunday school and church. Mrs. Kern or Mrs. Boles regularly passed out a supply of Bible cards, which had a picture on the front and the Golden Text (memory verse) and Bible lesson for the following Sunday on the back. By the time we got home from church, the noon passenger train had passed, and Dad had squandered a dime on a copy of the *Fort Worth Star Telegram*—and sometimes a second dime on the *Dallas Morning News*. This meant two sets of funny papers (who ever heard of a comic section?). Our favorite characters included Flip, who always wore a tin can for a hat, Maggie and Jiggs, Danny Dreamer, the Katzenjammer Kids, Mutt and Jeff, and, of course, Buster Brown and his bulldog, Tige.

After finishing the funny papers, we ate lunch. For a number of years, my family climbed the hill to visit Uncle Charlie and Aunt Rosa Felts and have the noon meal, or they came down to our place. On such Sundays, six boys enjoyed hilarious afternoons while the women disposed of dirty dishes and joined the men for domino games. We boys flitted from train and bank robbers, to Texas Rangers, to a band of Indians, to Indian scouts, to stagecoach driving. These games were much more fun at Uncle Charlie's, for he had a whole mountainside covered with trees and huge boulders to hide behind. Custer and his troops would never have been slaughtered at the Little Big Horn had they had the benefit of our counsel and expertise.

For years, Harry and I kept a twelve-foot-square tent in our yard. We could extend the tent another eight feet by raising one side, but it was seldom done. Inside the tent, the two Spratt boys slept on army cots most of the summer, protected from mosquito bites by oil of citronella smeared over exposed parts of the body. I never could decide which was the worse, mosquito bites or the odor of the oil. During the day, we converted the tent to a workshop where we made kites, toys, and military and Indian equipment.

We did wonders with gunnysacks. Our two cows, two horses, and poultry consumed sack after sack of chops and bran. As sacks accumulated we seized upon them, unraveled the seams, and obtained enough twine to sew and fashion the sacks into tepees, pup tents, or a maze of connecting rooms, or we could make Indian or cowboy regalia.

We played a lot of baseball. The baseballs we used had oilcloth covers stitched around a wad of cottonseed hulls, and one blow from the bat of an embryonic slugger could burst the cover and scatter the hulls all over the place. A much better ball cost a half dollar, but we saved these for important games. For practice and for scrub games, we generally used a homemade ball. We would wind a ball or two of twine tightly and stitch it round and round to keep it from unwinding—or we would stuff a wad of rags into the toe of an old sock and stitch the sock closed. A fair-sized pebble embedded in the rags gave it sufficient weight for throwing.

There were no coaches or organized sports in the Mingus Independent School District. There was not even a basketball backboard and basket. Thurber did have an outside basketball court. In both places, games at noon and at recess were more or less spontaneous. Thurber maintained a clubroom with all sorts of game facilities for the men, but it offered nothing for the schoolchildren.

As I grew older my interests changed. When we got electric lights, I did more reading in the evening. Few of the books could be classified as literature, good fiction, or history. *Black Beauty* came my way when a fifth-grade teacher ordered books for those children who would bring her fifty cents. Zane Grey's works were the most popular, and volume after volume passed from boy to boy. There was a scattering of books by G. A. Henty and Horatio Alger, and everyone read Harold Bell Wright between 1910 and 1920. I also read *Robinson Crusoe.*

One warm spring night, while sitting in the dining room reading a scary section of a book, I chanced to glance up. A heavy curtain separated our dining room and kitchen. As I watched, the left edge of the curtain moved slowly into the dining room about a foot, then dropped gently back in place. The movement was eerie, but I was a brave boy and resumed reading. When the curtain moved again, I closed the book and studied the curtain. It repeated the eerie movement several times. I was alone in the house and decided that Mother or Grandpa was having a bit of fun at my expense. I yelled, "Come on out from behind there, I know who you are!" I quit fooling around and headed for bed. The winter covers had not been stored, so I pulled them over my head.

Mother came in and wanted to know why I was in bed. I replied, "You know why." Then she asked why I had all of that cover over me and my clothes on. As the curtain was still performing its eerie dance, I got up and jerked it aside to find nothing but the kitchen. Gentle spring breezes can be deceptive—especially when a boy is reading *Robinson Crusoe* after dark.

Capt. William F. Drannan wrote two books about his thirty-one years on the plains and in the mountains as a trapper, chief of scouts, and Indian fighter. I once saw the captain ride his pony up to his booth at the county fair in Mineral Wells. He was dressed in fringed buckskins and Indian moccasins, sported long, flowing white hair, and wore a large Stetson hat. To me, he reeked of Indians, buffalo, and beaver. I read his books more than once. It was a terrible blow to learn years later that my hero was nothing but a damn liar. Some historian, a smart aleck authority on western history, had researched every episode related by Drannan and proved that everything he had written was false. The only thing he accepted as true was Drannan's statement that he had been born.*

Doctors have often been placed high on the sucker list, and Father was no exception. A book agent sold him on the cultural value of Dr. Charles W. Eliot's Five Foot Shelf of Books (*Harvard Classics*), and he bought the set. After he shelved them in his office, I went to work on the choicest volumes. No one else in the family touched them. While the culture bug was biting, Dad subscribed to a correspondence course on public speaking. He pursued the lessons diligently and became an effective speaker. He would even break the routine

---

*See W. N. Bate, *Frontier Legend: Texas Finale of Capt. William F. Drannan, Pseudo Frontier Comrade of Kit Carson.*—Ed.

benediction at the close of an all-day session of Baptist women by starting off, "Lord, have mercy on this lone old Methodist among all of these Baptists." A ten-volume set of *The World's Orators* came with the speaking course and I read them all.*

I also found interesting books when Mother, Harry, and I visited Aunt Callie Ross, Mother's older sister, and her family at Pecos during the summer. Uncle Bill and Aunt Callie had two or three bookcases filled with volumes that could entrance any boy, and while there I read my eyes out. As their three boys never read any of those books, I often wished some of them would be given to me, or that I would be told to take a few home to read, but that never happened.

Our visits to the Ross ranch were memorable. On boarding the train, the first thing we saw was the news butch who started down the aisle with an enticing basket of goodies. Mother headed off begging scenes by shaking her head as the butch approached. However, we usually helped him lighten his inventory before the trip ended. After we passed Big Spring the country grew windier and more desolate, and we invariably saw large prairie dog towns. Several of the little animals scurried here and there while others reared up atop mounds, as though interested in watching the train pass by. Roads were wagon trails that meandered across open country. The towns of Midland, Odessa, and Monahans were little more than general stores, section houses, and cattle pens and corrals.

The Ross ranch was sixty miles north of Pecos, in New Mexico.[†] Loving County and the town of Mentone lay between the two places, but only a native knew when he passed through Mentone. A branch of the Santa Fe Railroad ran north from the T&P line at Pecos through Carlsbad and Roswell, New Mexico, and a mixed train with several box and cattle cars and a passenger coach passed north and south on alternate days. The tracks were about ten miles west from the ranch house, so the women and kids usually rode the train up and were met by a hack from the ranch. After 1912 Uncle Bill had two automobiles, and we drove from Pecos to the ranch by car. There was no pavement.

Near the ranch house, three or four windmills ran constantly, that

---

*Guy Carleton Lee, ed., *The World's Orators* . . .

[†]William L. Ross (1865–1915) and Callie Felts Ross (1872–1955) were the parents of five children. In 1890 Ross, an ambitious young cowman, bought the remnants of the Hash Knife herd and established his headquarters at the old Dixieland place, north of Pecos. By 1901 Ross was running cattle on two hundred sections across the state line in New Mexico (Hughes, *Pecos*, pp. 20, 149, 303–306).—Ed.

is, if there was any wind. They poured streams of water into an earthen tank, with the overflow running through a six-inch pipe into a second tank. Elberta peach trees grew around the edges of these tanks, and our summer visits coincided with the peach season. For the better part of a week, we peeled, canned, and preserved peaches. Bushel after bushel filled quart and half-gallon jars. Mother and Aunt Callie supervised the cooking while everybody else, including most of the ranch hands, peeled and sliced. The cook had no difficulty preparing meals during this time, because the canning kept the oven hot during the day. Toward mealtime, he edged a large pan of steak between the preserving pots for frying and then a skillet for making a gallon of cream gravy. Breakfast preparations posed no problem, for the preserving process for the day had not begun.

When the trees had been stripped of their fruit, the ranch hands returned to the chores of rounding up, branding calves, castrating, and separating the animals for different pastures. During the castrating, the crew pitched mountain oysters into buckets,* and the ranch cook later roasted them on the hot coals remaining from the branding fires. The women saw that mountain oyster suppers were restricted to the men and eaten in the branding pens. If the summer was exceptionally dry, and grass at the water tanks near the ranch house became scarce, everybody, including the kids, mounted saddle horses to collect and drive the stock eight or ten miles west to the Pecos River, where grass and water were plentiful. When the cattle were moving quietly toward the river, the women and the cook rode back to the house to get the evening meal under way.

Uncle Bill kept one or two cowboys on hand to break broncs. They were good at their business and seldom ran into trouble. On one occasion, however, a buster was thrown and suffered a brain concussion. With the closest doctor sixty miles away, there was considerable concern on the ranch for two or three days. Fortunately, within a week he was able to ride again. Cowboys also periodically rode out to mend fence, carrying a combination wire cutter and hammer, a coil of barbed wire, and a bag of staples with them. On one occasion, the report came to the ranch that a buffalo had drifted in from nowhere. Approaching a barbed wire fence, the animal simply had lowered his head and increased his gait to a trot and cleared a strip of fence along with several fence posts. For a time, the fence riders

---

*Mountain oysters are available at the spring and fall roundups when bull calves are castrated. Stella Hughes (*Chuck Wagon Cookin'*, pp. 30–31, 108) describes the preparation and frying of these range delicacies.

added a post-hole digger to their mending gear. Nobody ever said, but I am sure that the poor buffalo bit the dust when a Winchester or a Colt-44 barked at him.

The prettiest sight at the ranch was when a thousand or more blue quail gathered outside the corrals in late evening to feed on the grain Uncle Bill had scattered out for them. He would have thrown anybody off the place who dared to shoot a quail within five miles of the ranch house. As the summer drew to a close, we headed back to Mingus.

Every fall we looked forward to hunting season. To people on small farms, a deer was a predator, and if one visited a vegetable garden or a grain field more than two or three nights in succession, it quickly ended up as venison in the farmer's smokehouse. Likewise, the wild turkey could easily become part of a turkey and dressing dinner. From season to season, farmers also killed or trapped foxes and wolves as insurance against loss of poultry or young livestock. Rabbits and squirrels were plentiful, as were duck, doves, and quail.

Hunting had its comical and near-tragic sides. On one occasion an Italian miner from Thurber raced his buggy to Dad's office, jumped out and rushed in, yelling, "Mr. Doctor! Mr. Doctor! Come queek! Come queek! A man so seek, he 'bout to die!" Dad calmed the fellow down, jotted down the house number on Italian Hill where the sick man was confined, then got in his buggy and started for Thurber at a trot.

He found a very sick man when he entered the home. The patient was spasmodically trying to vomit from a stomach long since empty. Dad asked a few questions and then wanted to know what the fellow had eaten. The reply was, "Nothing, Mr. Doctor." He repeated the question a few more times, then brusquely demanded a straight answer. That finally got results. The sick man had gone hunting a day or two earlier, killed a blackbird, brought it home, and eaten it. The doctor asked to see the feathers of the blackbird and was led to the trash pile at the rear of the house. There in all their ebony glory were the feathers of a buzzard. The man recovered, but Dad always wondered what kept him from dying.

Kin Pemberton was an old bachelor cousin of Mother's who for many years lived on his four-section ranch several miles southwest of Thurber. Kin wore white hair flowing almost to his neck, a white handlebar mustache, a small goatee, and a large gray western Stetson, and would easily have passed for a true Kentucky colonel. We had rather see Cousin Kin come for a visit than to see Santa Claus, for he was a barrel of fun. Every fall we looked forward to a hunting trip on his ranch. As he lived within several hours' drive, we could leave in the surrey when school was out and reach his place about dark.

The family drove out one year on Wednesday before Thanksgiving. While Kin and Dad fed and curried the horse, Mother fixed supper. After the meal, the men settled down to a couple of cigars. Dad wanted to know how Kin had been. "Wal, Jawn," said Kin in his best nasal twang, "I waz right puny up 'til about two weeks ago. Jist didn't have any pep. Then I begin to take some of that stuff I got here, and now I'm feelin' fust rate." The doctor wanted to see what the stuff was. Kin went over to a small box sitting on the hearth beside the fireplace, dug around a bit, and came out with a pint bottle which he handed to "Jawn." Dad read the label aloud, "Lydia E. Pinkham's Vegetable Compound."

The women's remedy must have cured Kin of all his ailments. In spite of the bitter cold, he was up before daylight next morning helping with breakfast, so we could be at a good-sized earthen tank by daylight for ducks. The best way to shoot ducks was to crawl quietly up on the dam and peer cautiously over the top to see where the birds were. Dad, Kin, Harry, and I reached the tank just about daylight. The two men had guns, the boys were novices acting as observers and retrievers. Spotting ducks on the tank, the men began shooting. When it was over, three or four ducks were floating on the water and five or six were scattered over the ground. We all remained still and quiet for a few minutes until it was clear that the birds would not return.

As Harry and I retrieved the birds on the ground, the men discussed how to get the birds in the water. They commented on the brisk north wind and knew the temperature was well below freezing. Hunting was great sport, but its primary object was to provide food. Hunters never abandoned dead game if there was a way to recover it. We had no dog to bring in the dead ducks, the boys were poor swimmers, and Kin was too old to risk it.

Dad decided that he was elected. We gathered a big pile of dead brush and set it afire. Dad shucked his clothes and waded in and started swimming. Fortunately, he did not take the cramps. He brought in two birds against his chest the first trip and got the other two on the next run. By that time, we had the fire blazing at least ten feet high. The swimmer toasted himself on one side and then the other for twenty minutes before he stopped shaking and his teeth quit chattering. We then went back to the house. Dad stuck close to the fireplace to drive out the rest of the chill until the noon meal was ready.

That afternoon the four of us took off again, this time in search

of quail. The men did the shooting and the boys again acted as retrievers. We were good at it. When we saw a bird fall, we glued our
eyes to the spot and went after the game. By late afternoon we had
a good supply of quail, as well as two or three rabbits that had made
the mistake of seeking another hiding place when the hunters were
stalking quail.

I was not allowed to shoot a gun until I was twelve. Dad then
handed me his gun to try on a jackrabbit. I killed it, but my shooting
average was never good. Through the year, we usually had squirrel,
young jackrabbits, and cottontails as welcome changes from the
standard diet of salt pork. We often drove out into the country in
the late afternoon for rabbits, and sometimes spent a morning or an
afternoon hunting squirrel. We seldom came back empty-handed.
But when I learned that one could catch rabbit fever from skinning a
rabbit, I never killed one to eat thereafter.

In the late fall, when the weather turned cold, Mother dug out our
winter clothes. Whistling winds often accompanied the cold snaps,
driving the chill from ten to thirty degrees below the thermometer
reading. This was the time of year when I exchanged my American
Beauties for store-bought long drawers. We had a ready supply of
warm clothing. Grandma Felts kept us supplied with mittens, and
Mother crocheted or knitted caps, socks, and earmuffs. And every
few years Aunt Callie knitted Dad a pair of house shoes with fleece
inner soles. One night a pair suffered a disaster when Dad went out
during a thunderstorm to close the cellar door. There was no light
and Dad, feeling his way along the side of the house, approached a
washtub placed to collect rainwater and took an extra long step. He
miscalculated and stepped in the middle of the flooded tub. Cussing
Louisa and her damned water tubs, he finished his trip and closed
the door. He put the wet shoe under the heater to dry out, and the
next morning the innersole had shrunk to half the length of his foot.

Outside work called for special clothing. Everybody had a pair of
overshoes (no one called them galoshes), with thick rubber soles and
felt tops equipped with buckles. All who had to be out in cold, rainy
weather wore long, yellow slickers and southwesters, together with
gumboots, or heavy lace boots, saturated with neat's foot oil. This
was standard regalia, whether on foot, horseback, or in a wagon.

In cold weather we attached curtains to buggies and surreys. One
curtain fastened to the vehicle top and extended out over the dashboard. The reins passed through a slit. There also was an isinglass
window about eight inches square on the driver's side. For travel
about town or to Thurber, we had one or more heavy lap robes, and
on bitterly cold days Mother heated large stones or bricks, wrapped

them in a heavy cloth, and placed them on the floor of the vehicle and under the lap robe to warm feet and radiate heat. Some people even tried using kerosene lanterns under their robes, but the danger of fire kept such use to a minimum.

By early winter, life around home had settled into a regular routine. The lazy days of summer, the beginning of a new school year, and the first forays into the countryside to hunt faded into memory. Ahead lay the festive days of Thanksgiving and Christmas, when family and friends shared food, goodwill, and hope for a new year.

11. Holiday Seasons

THANKSGIVING, CHRISTMAS, and New Year's brought families and friends together to celebrate time-honored traditions in our community. Throughout the year, Sunday dinners were lavish, but none compared with special meals that were prepared on these occasions. It was a time when families and friends visited with each other and shared the holiday spirit. For some it was a time of rededication; for others it was a time to reminisce about holidays in the past. To all, young and old, the season meant gaiety, laughter, and a reaffirmation of love for one another.

Our family began preparations for Thanksgiving a month early and stayed busy until Christmas. We penned the turkeys and fed them extra rations of grain to ensure nice, fat birds. Mother stopped selling eggs and began storing them to meet the demands for extended baking. Fresh cranberries showed up in the grocery stores and we bought them by the gallon for homemade cranberry sauce. Pumpkins raised in our garden or in Grandpa Felts's were stewed and put aside for pies. Surplus butter sales stopped. For days before each special occasion, Mother baked extra-large pans of biscuits and saved the overage for dressing. Large patches of cornbread waited in readiness for the other half of the dressing. We pulled the tomato vines before frost and hung them in the cellar, where the green tomatoes would ripen by Thanksgiving. Leaves were picked off the sage plants in the garden for seasoning.

A few days before Thanksgiving, we added three extra leaves to the dining table, making it nine feet long by six wide. The best china, glasses, cut-glass bowls and dishes, and silverware came out of the china closet to be washed and polished. These had not been used since the previous Christmas. The old kitchen range worked overtime. Mother baked six pumpkin pies, several butter custards and egg custards, a pound cake, and at least one coconut layer cake. She tucked the turkey into the oven the day before the feast.

On the appointed morning of the anointed day, Mother prepared the dressing and while this cooked she dumped a half dozen vegetables into pans for heating and cooking. If a hog had been recently butchered, she added a large pot of fresh spareribs and dumplings made of either flour or cornmeal to the menu. In the absence of spareribs or backbone, she substituted hogshead pudding.

With the final spasm of cooking under way, other hands whipped cream, at least a quart, to dab on slices of pumpkin pie or dishes of home-canned peaches. We loaded beet pickles, bread and butter pickles, and pickled onions into dishes, and piled tomatoes, sliced celery, and cranberry sauce into others. As the tempo increased, one or two persons set the table, brewed coffee, made a large pitcher of punch, and placed glasses of milk at specified plates. When a large pan of biscuits appeared, Dad already had sliced the turkey and neatly arranged it on the platter.

As the hour hand approached two o'clock in the afternoon, and just before everyone dropped dead of starvation, the call came for the first table. This shift included the grown-ups and those under three. The real "young 'uns" continued to starve and spit cotton. Just as eternity neared its end, they too were called. The second crew wolfed down twice as much food in half the time taken by the first table.

After the hungry were fed, we tackled the aftermath. A boxcar load of pots, pans, dishes, glassware, and silver had to be washed and dried during the afternoon. A cake of homemade lye soap helped reduce the ordeal.

During the weeks before Christmas, my family often paid visits to friends in Mingus. There was one evening I still remember. Dad took the family to the home of Rosseau, the druggist, who rented a room to Bob Moreland, the school principal. As we sat around a potbellied stove, Bob edged into the conversation and told a story about a Christmas experience back in Tennessee as a child. Tilting back against the wall in a cane-bottomed chair, his heels hooked over the lower rung, the blue-eyed, bespectacled teacher smiled as he related "the Christmas I'll never forget."*

My mother died when I was born, and my father fell victim to typhoid fever before I was old enough to remember him. Grandma and Grandpa took me in. They had a farm not too far from Nashville, and there I grew up. They lived in a double-log

---

*A fuller version of this story appears in Spratt, "When Bob Threw Christmas Away," pp. 86–91.—Ed.

cabin joined by a covered hallway open at either end. The cabins had been built sometime prior to the Civil War. Trips to town were rare, possibly not more than three or four times a year.

Life on an eastern Tennessee farm in 1885 hadn't changed much since 1785. We never had much money but always plenty of food for man, fowl, and beast, all of it we raised. I was a little tyke when the farm became my home, but there were chores for me. I helped gather eggs and feed the poultry, and received other assignments as I grew older. There was wood to chop, cows to milk, livestock to feed, plowing to be done, fruits and berries to be picked, and hogs to be butchered. There was also cotton to chop three or four months a year. During the summer, the Methodists and Baptists usually broke our routine with camp meetings, but the two big days of the year were Thanksgiving and Christmas, with Thanksgiving coming in a poor second.

Christmas was the day of days, especially for the young 'uns. That was the day old Santa filled stockings to overflowing and around the fireplace piled toys, fruits, and nuts that not even Aladdin's Lamp could produce. Christmas at Grandpa Moreland's was as grandiose and exciting as any.

He and Grandma had a daughter who lived in Nashville and she had two boys. Two or three days before Christmas, this aunt and my two cousins would appear at the farm, and the two women would busy themselves with preparations for Christmas dinner. Hams were baked to a golden brown, pumpkin and molasses pies appeared in bunches, the "fixins" for turkey dressing were readied, and peach pickles came from the cellar. Nothing was spared in making ready for a real feast.

We three boys always were sent to bed early on Christmas Eve. Early to bed meant early to rise. I was usually up between four and four-thirty next morning, and hurried to get a fire throwing enough light to see what Santa had left. The flash of shiny red on the floor might be an iron train, or a fire engine, piled atop new clothing. Clothes never merited a second glance unless there was a pair of red-top, brass-toed boots or a Dave Crockett coonskin in the mess. Then for the stockings.

Holding a stocking for a quick spill, out rolled a couple of oranges, something seen only at Christmas or when someone in the family had a spell of pneumonia. Then came a jackknife with three blades (not an ordinary two-blader), a green top, peppermint and crinkled ribbon candy, niggertoes, almonds, English walnuts and two sticks of licorice. The other stocking might be garnished with a real coconut, another orange, followed by a cap pistol in all its silvery splendor, and then box after box of caps. The junk that followed—who cared!

Those Christmas seasons were gala ones. That is, all of them save one. On that one, when I was ten or eleven, it was nothing but gloom. Snow began falling about the middle of December and it snowed right up to Christmas day. Grandma didn't have a chance to get to town for Christmas shopping. That disturbed me. Like all sophisticated boys my age, I knew there wasn't any Santa Claus other than Grandma. My aunt came out with the boys at about the usual time, and she and Grandma started preliminary preparations for Christmas dinner. The nearer December 25th came, the gloomier I grew. I could see nothing but empty stockings for me. There was only one consoling thought. Maybe there really was a Santa Claus. Sometimes one and sometimes the other line of thought took over. They swept me from hope to despair and back again.

On Christmas Eve Granny and Auntie spent the morning frying doughnuts. That night we three boys were shunted to bed in the early evening after hanging up six stockings. That gave me a ray of hope. At four next morning I crawled out of my trundle bed and headed for the fireplace. In a matter of seconds I had a big bed of coals dug out of the ashes and was throwing first small then large logs over them. The bed of coals gave enough light for me to see there had been no overflow from the stockings—that was bad. But I could tell that my stockings had been filled—that was good.

As the first blaze crackled through the logs, I reached for a stocking. It was filled with doughnuts. I dropped it like it had bit me and reached for the other—suspecting the worst. It was more doughnuts. I mustered all the disgust I could put in one word and let it explode, "Doughnuts! Who wants doughnuts for Christmas? I'm gonna' throw 'em in the fire!" Then came Grandma's voice from the big bed in the corner, "No you aren't, Bobby!" "I am, too." Then came her quiet warning, "If you do, I'll thrash you." But I wasn't fully cornered, not yet. "Well, if I can't burn 'em, I'm gonna throw 'em out." "You can throw 'em out if you wish, but don't you dare throw a single doughnut in the fire."

By this time I was in a white fury. I grabbed both stockings and headed for the door. I took a stocking by the toe and gave my arm a swing, planting a half-circle of doughnuts in the snow. The other stocking received the same treatment. By this time my cousins were up and examining their stockings. They were filled with an array of bright toys (Auntie always brought their Christmas along when they came out from town). This added insult to injury. I sat in the corner and sulked, getting madder by the minute.

Granny and Auntie, meantime, had crossed the hall to the other cabin and were preparing breakfast. Granny called to me to come and eat. I told her I didn't want anything, that I wasn't hungry. "Suit yourself," she said, "It's here for you, but if you don't want it there's more for the rest of us." The others ate. Afterwards, the women cleaned up the kitchen.

It was well up into the morning before Grandma came back to the cabin where I was. I hadn't moved from my corner, and my sulk had grown deeper. She crossed the room, took her shawl from a peg, flipped it over her shoulders, then told me to come with her. We went to the door from which I had planted my doughnuts and out into the yard. Granny hunkered down and began to scratch away snow where the crust had been broken. Soon a doughnut appeared. This she repeated four times.

As she swept away snow the fifth time, no doughnut was there. Instead, a shiny silver dollar appeared. I made a grab for it but she already had it palmed. "Give it to me! It's mine!" I remonstrated. "No, Bobby, it was yours but you threw it away," she said. "Now it's mine." She made a few more scratches and a second dollar came out of the snow. We repeated our previous conversation. Grandma did not play games. She didn't give me those dollars after she thought I had been taught my lesson. She kept them.

Those were the biggest dollars I ever saw and at that time I could have bought half of Nashville with them. One thing I'll tell you, from that day to this anything a person gave me I've taken an' said, "Much oblige." That was the biggest Christmas I ever had—but I threw it away.

Christmas Day at the Spratts opened with an assault on the stockings. A skimpy breakfast followed. By midmorning, Mother appeared with a punch bowl of eggnog sporting thick cream, eggs, sugar, and a cupful or two of whiskey. A tray of homemade sugar cookies garnished with green and red candy-coated spices rested nearby.

Later in the day, we tackled Christmas dinner. A favorite was mincemeat pies. When the top pie was eaten, the next one was sliced. Mother always added a tablespoonful of whiskey to each pie, contending that it provided a better flavor than the same amount of vanilla extract. Dad was fond of cranberry and raisin pie, so she made one or two of them for him. Homemade peach pickles replaced canned peaches, and candied yams shoved aside creamed potatoes or potato salad. For this occasion, we ate on the long linen tablecloth and used linen napkins. Roast turkey, dressing, giblet gravy, and cranberry sauce appeared. The cycle of two tables and extended dishwashing repeated the Thanksgiving arrangement.

New Year's Eve was an important event for us, too. We stayed awake until midnight, eating pies and cakes left over from Christmas and making large batches of popcorn in a screen popper held over the bed of coals in the heater. We dumped each fresh batch into a large crock and stirred it around in a mixture of melted butter and salt. A gallon or so of fruit punch quenched our thirst. For some reason, with all of her superstitions, Mother never cooked the traditional mess of black-eyed peas for this occasion. While munching cake, pie, and popcorn and sipping juice, the family played dominoes, forty-two, pitch, or Rook. We saved the fireworks that Santa had left for New Year's Eve, especially skyrockets and Roman candles.

As the clock approached midnight, we stopped the games and prepared to blast out the old year and welcome the new one. Harry and I shoveled out a few coals to set off our fireworks, and Dad dragged out his old Colt 41. At the first stroke of midnight, every whistle in the country screamed—at the mines, on locomotives, at the Thurber power plant, and at the carshops in Mingus. Dad and other men went out in the yard and fired pistols or shotguns while Harry and I set off Roman candles and skyrockets, as did many other kids in town. Friends and neighbors yelled "Happy New Year" to each other, and now and then someone rendered an off-key version of "Auld Lang Syne."

In those days, these celebrations generally involved two or three families or close friends. The churches may have hosted "watch parties," but I cannot recall any. The same was true for the fraternal orders. Over in Thurber, the Texas & Pacific Mercantile and Manufacturing Company celebrated with a lavish New Year's Eve Ball. This was the major social event of the year for the company. In Mingus, however, New Year's Eve celebrations were principally family affairs that honored age-old customs and traditions.

12. Passing Trains

I N THE early 1900s, those families whose homes sat within one
hundred yards of the main line of a transcontinental railroad were
to be envied. True, they had to endure noise, smoke, cinders, and
coal dust, but these nuisances were more than offset by certain ad-
vantages. Watching the trains—freight, passenger, specials, circus,
and military—roll by to the east and west over a period of years was
like seeing an endless stream of life. As our house was near the
tracks in Mingus, we enjoyed the constantly changing world created
by passing trains.

As a kid, I was fascinated by the railroad. I recall watching switch
engines shunt cars loaded with crushed ballast, piles of creosoted
crossties, and heavy rails onto sidings. Work gangs followed, rebuild-
ing the roadbed for heavier, longer, and faster trains. A few years
later, the cycle was repeated. Heavier rails and ties were laid, and
larger spikes driven to clinch the ribbons of steel. Section hands
periodically patrolled the tracks, spending long hours checking the
roadbed and cleaning the right-of-way.

Railroad cars changed, too. The first cars I remember were huge
boxes mounted on flanged wheels that jolted and bounced at every
turn of the axle. More than half of those bearing the T&P symbol
carried cattle or coal. The coal company dispatched over 120 cars of
coal each day from Mingus six days a week. Other cars left town
loaded with sand, gravel, or crushed stone. After oil replaced coal,
these gondolas carried pipe, and on several occasions I saw an engine
purposely bump a car to jar the pipe off the body of a hobo who had
been crushed to death while riding on the shifting cargo. For years,
many freight trains from the west were loaded with bawling cattle.
Each time one stopped in Mingus, and they all did, a cowpuncher
climbed down from the caboose carrying a long pole. He inspected
the cars for fallen cattle, and when he found a steer down, he punched,
jabbed, and pried until the animal got to its feet. These cars moved

east loaded, but returned west as empties. Once in a great while, a car would be jammed with hogs, and sometimes sheep were shipped in cattle cars that had been converted into double-deckers.

For years, the T&P used wooden tank cars. They resembled large cylinders and served to haul water to distant storage tanks. These cars grew fewer as the railroad built more water facilities along its main line, then disappeared entirely from the local scene when the T&P created a lake by throwing a dam across Gibson Creek at Mingus. Steel tank cars appeared around 1912, when Bob Loflin became the local distributor-dealer for the Magnolia Petroleum Company. The company erected two 10,000-gallon storage tanks and shipped in fuel to fill Loflin's business needs. One tank contained gasoline and the other kerosene. There were few automobiles around Mingus, but practically everyone used kerosene for fuel and light. When the T&P brought in the Ranger oil fields in 1917, it began a desperate search for oil tank cars. It managed to procure the needed cars, but I well recall seeing a few old cylindrical wood cars loaded with Ranger oil rattling along the tracks.

When revolution swept Mexico and border incidents occurred, the U.S. government used the railroads to move soldiers to the danger zone. Many of these troop trains passed through Mingus. The movement of men and military equipment increased sharply, when Gen. John J. "Black Jack" Pershing was ordered to lead a punitive expedition into Mexico to end the depredations of Pancho Villa.* As Mingus was a railroad division point, most of the military trains stopped there for fuel, water, and orders. This gave the kids a chance to look over a train and talk with some of the personnel.

Seeing real soldiers close at hand was quite a novelty in 1916. At the State Fair in Dallas I had watched an army engineer unit race a wagon loaded with heavy lumber to the middle of the racetrack, erect a bridge, gallop a three-inch cannon and caisson over the structure, then whirl and unlimber the gun and fire a blank shell in mock destruction of the bridge. I also had seen cavalry units at drill as we passed military posts by train between Sierra Blanca and El Paso and stared at a few that lolled around depots. But seeing and talking with soldiers en route to war was something else. At this time, the armed

---

*Revolution swept Mexico in 1910, and as warring factions violated its borders, the United States began a troop build-up there. Following Pancho Villa's March 1916 raid on Columbus, New Mexico, Pres. Woodrow Wilson sent Gen. John J. Pershing and a cavalry column into Mexico to capture Villa. His mission proved unsuccessful (Frank E. Vandiver, *Black Jack: The Life and Times of John J. Pershing*, chap. 17).—Ed.

forces called up were primarily national guardsmen, and many adults branded them a pretty sorry lot, but they were heroes to every boy.

The troop trains varied little in their composition. The men wore olive drab and carried Springfield rifles, 1890 issue. They also had machine guns, but their field wagons and caissons might well have seen service at Gettysburg. The train generally included several box-cars loaded with horses and mules and flatcars carrying wagons and artillery, all tied down securely. Baggage cars served as kitchens, with military field stoves installed in each. The army was still a meat-and-potato outfit, so preparation of mess was not complicated. The troops rode in tourist-type pullmans, with a regular pullman for officers. A caboose followed at the rear, because the trains were clas-sified as freights. Huge letters chalked on the sides of the cars warned Villa of his impending fate.

The men usually remained in the coaches while the train was standing in Mingus. However, if they had been riding for twenty-four hours without exercise, the commanding officers ordered them to detrain. They fell in as squads and companies and marched about town for fifteen to thirty minutes before reboarding. I saw no motor-ized equipment or military airplanes. In fact, this was only a short time after the army had turned down the Wright Brothers' effort to interest it in a plane. The Mexican episode was a prelude to our in-volvement in World War I.

The impact of the Great War of 1917 on every facet of American life far exceeded anything in our prior history. The nation's actual participation came about slowly. I was in Fort Worth five months after we declared war in April and saw carpenters begin work on what became Camp Bowie. Six months later I went back there to watch the Thirty-sixth Division march down Main Street before entraining for the East Coast and Europe. These men had started their training in the manual of arms with wooden guns. What hap-pened at Fort Worth had been repeated all over the United States. By the spring and summer of 1918, the country was alive with troop movements.

As railroads under private management broke down, the govern-ment took over their operation.* Prior to this, I had never seen a lo-comotive of another railroad on the T&P track, except when wash-outs near Sierra Blanca forced the Southern Pacific briefly to use the T&P line to Fort Worth. Now with government operation, loco-

---

*The federal government took over the nation's railroads in late December of 1917. The railroads in Texas were returned to private ownership on March 1, 1920 (Reed, *Texas Railroads*, pp. 724–725).

motives from the New York Central, Pennsylvania, and other roads appeared on the T&P. The government eliminated the hoarding of rolling stock and started shuttling cars and locomotives from one part of the country to another. As a result, a steady stream of troops and military equipment, in addition to huge quantities of food for Allied countries, passed through Mingus.

Troop trains in 1917 were different from those three or four years earlier. Helmets and trench or service caps had pushed aside the peaked-top brown campaign hat. Instead of horses and mules and military field wagons, we saw motor trucks riding on flatcars. Later in the war, the army moved several small tanks here and there, more for the public to see than anything else.

Local train traffic became crowded. In the fall of 1918, I attended high school at Weatherford, riding the train home and back once or twice a month. The cars were packed. On the day or night train, going or coming, I had to squeeze in among the other standees in the vestibule or ride in the aisle of the coach. I never found a seat on one of the trips. The T&P could not add coaches because they were in constant service for the military.

Special trains shuttled about the country boosting Liberty Bond sales. They generally carried a gondola car or two loaded with the wreckage of German planes, flatcars with captured enemy artillery and shells lobbed into Allied lines, and large posters depicting the vicious enemy. One flatcar carried a huge shell with a placard stating, "400 mm German Artillery Shell." A middle-aged fellow gawking with the rest of the crowd stopped at the big shell, read the caption, then exclaimed in deep astonishment, "My God! Four hundred miles a minute!" In a pullman car, clerks registered local bond sales. Several Allied soldiers, dressed in highly decorated uniforms and crippled by wounds, told audiences how the savage Hun was responsible for their losing an arm or leg.

The railroad enjoyed its heyday during these years. Beginning in 1916, American railroads began moving over one billion tons of freight annually, surpassing all previous records. When I entered the University of Texas at Austin in the fall of 1920, practically everyone rode trains if traveling any distance. The Missouri, Kansas & Texas ("Katy") Railroad solicited students just before Christmas, mailing letters describing the cost of round-trip tickets from Austin. A second letter came about three weeks before the close of the spring term advertising the same service. The Missouri Pacific offered a $1.50 round-trip weekend excursion rate from Austin to San Antonio, and many people, especially University of Texas students, took advantage of it.

In my youth, passenger trains included coaches fitted out as railway post offices. They did not stop at every station, but still picked up and delivered the mail. In small towns, the depot agent suspended a mail pouch between two arms extending horizontally from a small derricklike structure adjacent to the tracks. As the train flew by, an iron arm extending from the door of the mail car snared the pouch. The impact triggered a release and both arm and bag dropped to a vertical position. The clerk reached out and pulled the pouch into the car. To deliver the mail, the railway clerk kicked the pouch from the open car door as the train sped by the depot.

Firemen also snared travel orders on the fly. At the approach of a train, the telegraph operator went out and stood near the tracks, holding up a large hoop of light wood. To the hoop he clamped a set of travel orders. Seeing the telegrapher, the fireman climbed down on the steps at the rear of the cab and with his arm hooked the loop, jerked the orders loose, and tossed the hoop to the ground as the train passed the depot.

Times soon changed. The railroad's shift to oil-burning locomotives doomed the coal chutes along the line, and diesel fuel gradually drove water tanks into oblivion. Diesel locomotives did away with the need for fire knockers, boilermakers, machinists, and other specialists who kept steam locomotives in repair, as well as the roundhouses where men worked on these engines. The evolution of railroad locomotives virtually destroyed such towns as Toyah, Mingus, and Baird.

After World War I, the railroads altered freight cars to fit the changes in the goods they hauled. For example, the refrigerator car cooled by ice gradually passed from the scene. In the early days, these yellow cars moving east with California fruit had to be re-iced repeatedly. El Paso had a long icing platform, and all eastbound trains carrying fruit, whether Southern Pacific or Texas & Pacific, stopped there. The T&P also had facilities at Big Spring, Fort Worth, and various points in East Texas. At each station, one or more long chutes, built of two-by-twelve-inch boards and resting on a trestle as high as the cars, ran from a storage unit down to the tracks. Some chutes were several hundred feet long. Once a refrigerator car was in position, the dock crew started pushing three-hundred-pound blocks of ice down these chutes and into open vents at either end of the car. To cool a long fruit train, tons and tons of ice were required. Ice plants along the line enjoyed a profitable business. But when the railroads devised a belt system run by the axle of the car to power freezing units, mechanical refrigeration replaced the ice chutes.

Most railroads ran special trains from time to time. Perhaps the most famous I saw was Teddy Roosevelt's three-car special, which came through Mingus. Specials generally were set up for nonrepeat events, but others ran year after year. For example, the T&P advertised weekend specials during the major fairs. For both the State Fair in Dallas and the Fort Worth Fat Stock Show, the railroad added extra coaches to move the fairgoers. As the Fat Stock Show was held in early March then, Dad always went down, for he liked to buy an Irish shamrock for each member of the family. Sometimes he picked up an Irish pipe made of white clay, and once or twice he managed three Irish green hats (Mother had to be content with her shamrock). I am sure there is little Irish blood in the family, but he liked to pretend there was.

We may have ridden a special train when Dad took the family to El Paso with him about 1912, although as a railroad physician, he enjoyed free passes on the T&P. Dad was a delegate to the State Democratic Convention. I remember the long ride west, seeing the alligators in the downtown plaza in El Paso and, above all, meeting "Cyclone" Davis.* The four of us were eating breakfast when a tall, slender, gray-haired man finished his meal at an adjoining table and came over, extended his hand to Dad, and said, "Davis, is the name. 'Cyclone,' they call me." I knew nothing about "Cyclone" Davis, and probably cared less about him, but I did think that any man named "Cyclone" must be quite a whirlwind. Davis was a prominent Texas politician at the time.

Other special trains passed through Mingus. For years, I saw two all-pullman trains annually speed through Mingus about daylight heading west. These trains bore the Metropolitan Opera Company. I knew little about the company, except they were supposed to be great singers. They had to be great indeed to travel from Dallas or Fort Worth to California by pullman, accompanied by baggage cars carrying stage scenery and instruments for their orchestra. And occasionally we spotted a large carnival train loaded with rides, tents, gambling equipment, and personnel. Smaller shows traveled in one or two boxcars and a flatcar hitched to a freight, with the personnel riding curled up on the freight cars or separately on a passenger train.

Circus trains created great excitement. Buffalo Bill Cody's Wild West Show, Col. Zack Miller's 101 Ranch Circus, Hegenbach-Wallace

---

*James H. "Cyclone" Davis (1853–1940), an attorney and lecturer for the Farmers Alliance, served in the U.S. House of Representatives from 1915 to 1917 (Webb, *Handbook of Texas*, I, 470).—Ed.

Wild Animal Circus, Cole Brothers Circus, Clyde Beatty Circus, and of course Ringling Brothers, all traveled by rail in several sections (trains). Ringling Brothers required four sections. For some reason, they all seemed to be heading eastward when they passed through Mingus. They had performed in Abilene the previous night and were bound for Fort Worth to put on afternoon and night shows. In my early years, a circus occasionally stopped in Weatherford and put on a performance, but when the Model T became fairly common, this ended.

When a circus train stopped in Mingus for twenty or thirty minutes to take on coal (or oil) and water and allow the crew to eat breakfast, the town kids quickly gathered to inspect each section. Examining a circus train was the next best thing to seeing the show. Each section had flatcars, animal cars, and sleeping and dining coaches. A row of bright circus wagons sat on the flatcars, each firmly chocked to the bed. Wagon tongues had been removed and stowed beneath. Other wagons were loaded with tent parts, side poles and stakes, and main poles.

As a rule, the first section carried the dining tent and the mobile kitchen. Here also rode a set of wagons painted in red, gold, green, and yellow. The sides and ends were covered, for they contained the cages of the wild animals not used in the main tent performances. Next came the animal cars, which had giraffes, camels, zebras, dromedaries, and work horses that moved the wagons to and from the circus grounds. There was at least one sleeping car in this section, but many roustabouts curled up on bundles of canvas on the flatcars, while animal caretakers slept between the wagon cages or on the animal cars.

Performing animals—lions, tigers, dogs, horses, and elephants—rode in the second and third sections. The fourth section carried the main tent and many of the circus personnel. The sleeping cars ranged in quality according to the importance of the persons who rode in them. We tried to guess what great circus clown, aerial artist, acrobat, or tightwire artist lay sleeping in those bright red coaches. But the cars and cars of elephants perhaps drew the most attention. Many kids got closer views of these giants than they had ever had before. One or two elephants always managed to stand between the two huge doors in the centers of the cars, waving their trunks in the hope someone would pitch them peanuts or a handful of straw.

By the 1920s changes in railroading spelled doom to many small towns. Mingus went from 140 employees to none. Some of these people found other railroad employment of one kind or another, but a majority sought an alternate line of work or joined the ranks of the unemployed. Men who had been in the carshops became carpenters. As always, unskilled workers were hardest hit. When towns lost a sizable portion of their populations as a result of technological changes in railroad operations, men not only lost their jobs, but also their homes. A way of life began drawing to an end.

13. Thurber and Mingus Go into Decline

During World War I, the Thurber-Mingus district enjoyed unprecedented prosperity. The outbreak of hostilities in Europe in 1914 set the stage for growing industrial efforts to meet overseas demands for goods. The U.S. entry into the conflict in April of 1917 stimulated the production of coal and the need for increased railroad services. Work was plentiful and few people gave a second thought to events around them. Yet during these busy years, the winds of change were sweeping the land. Twenty miles to the west, at Ranger, the T&P opened a lucrative oil field that vitally affected the destiny of the Thurber district.

In the spring of 1917 every community in the land was caught up in the war spirit. As radio or wireless was used primarily in military communication, and the telephone was confined to local calls, distant news came over the wires in Morse code, and the general public received it in hometown newspapers. The government also made an effort to keep the public informed through a network of Four-Minute Speakers,* who daily received digests of up-to-the-minute news and made announcements in public places. Thousands of the speakers delivered short messages between film changes in motion picture houses across the country. A majority stayed within their time limit, but some rambled on for fifteen or twenty minutes.

In Mingus, as in most towns and hamlets, women organized groups to help the war effort. European winters were cold, so mothers, sisters, and sweethearts learned to knit and soon were producing woolen socks, sweaters, hoods, and mittens for the boys overseas. These same women met at churches and in private homes to roll bandages. They served in place of Red Cross units, which did not exist in small towns then. To raise money for their projects, the women

---

*The Texas Council of Defense kept a staff of "four-minute men" on call (Richardson et al., *Texas*, p. 316).—Ed.

put on local entertainment and gave ice cream or box suppers. Families saved quarters to buy thrift stamps, which could be exchanged for bonds, and observed the government's request for weekly meatless and wheatless days. When the Germans started using poison gas, the Allies called for millions of gas masks. Charcoal from coconuts had the greatest absorbent power against these gases, with peach seeds the next best item. Home canners began saving peach seeds, depositing them in collection barrels at strategic sites in town. Volunteers made periodic pickups and shipped these seeds to companies with ovens making charcoal for gas masks.

A profound love of country was manifested everywhere. Top composers and writers turned their talents to patriotic airs, and we soon were singing a multitude of war songs. "Over There" may have topped the list, but we also sang "Good-bye Broadway, Hello France," "He Was Just a Long Lean Country Gink," "It's a Long Way to Tipperary," and many others. Sir Harry Lauder's "The Laddies That Fought and Won," in tribute to the doughboys and the Tommies, also was popular in this country.* Vaudeville and stage shows emphasized patriotic themes. Chautauquas provided speakers and engaged home economics teachers and home demonstration agents to counsel families on preparing meatless and wheatless dishes. Communities by the thousands sponsored an endless procession of amateur musicals to help the war effort. Some entrepreneur doubtless made a small fortune when he began printing tiny American flags on gummed paper, for most men decorated their stiff white collars with these flags. Members of the Royal Air Force introduced Americans to the swagger stick, and many a young swain sported this mark of distinction.

Teams canvassed the country, promoting the sale of Liberty Bonds.†
Meetings in each community were well publicized. Everybody attended and practically all bought a bond of some denomination. Every absentee was noted, especially if he were a local businessman or banker. He was immediately classed as a "slacker" and could

---

*Harry MacLennon Lauder (1870–1950) was a famous Scottish singer and songwriter who made his debut in London in 1900. Dressed in kilts and carrying a twisted walking stick, he became a leading comic, making many tours of the United States during World War I (Gladys Malvern, *Valiant Minstrel: The Story of Sir Harry Lauder*, song 201).—Ed.

†In May of 1917, Texas set up a State Council of Defense, with 240 county councils and 15,000 community councils, to spur the sale of Liberty Bonds and promote the war effort (Richardson et al., *Texas*, pp. 315–316). —Ed.

easily expect that a generous application of yellow paint would be applied to his front door and front gate. This was an invitation for the Death Angel to strike. Boycotts of his business might follow.

Communities not only demanded attendance at local bond drives, but almost dictated the sales. A prominent citizen might go to a meeting intending to purchase a five-hundred-dollar bond, but wind up with a ten-thousand-dollar bond. During a meeting, he quickly became aware of what the community felt he could afford. Small-town bankers who preferred to put their money in mortgages or vendor lien notes contracted to buy sizable Liberty Bonds. Community pressure had as much, or more, to do with the success of these drives than any directive from Washington.

Patriotism demanded conformity. Suggesting that a person was a draft evader, a "slacker," was ten times more insulting than calling him an obscene name. This was brought home to me when I appeared in a high school play. Oma Link, my speech teacher at Strawn, produced a patriotic drama with an American soldier as the hero. We performed at Strawn, Mingus, and Thurber, and planned to move to Gordon, when the boy who played the hero in the play was ordered overseas with his outfit. I had played the role and agreed to fill in for him.

I knew the part well, but for some reason missed one of the last rehearsals. The manager of the Mingus lumberyard, a Gordon resident, met me on the street next day with the greeting, "You're a slacker, you missed rehearsal last night." Smarting from the accusation, I reported the remark to Father. Somehow Uncle Charlie Felts got hold of the story, too. Dad and I located the manager, and with Uncle Charlie arriving on the scene, I asked the man why he called me a slacker. He quickly explained that members of the cast had kiddingly called anyone who missed a rehearsal a slacker. He apologized profusely and we were satisfied. Calling someone a slacker could provoke a fight and draw blood. Actually, in Mingus I knew of no one who evaded the draft.

In the fall of 1917, the T&P struck oil at Ranger,* twenty miles to the west, and a mad rush followed. Roughnecks, teamsters, gamblers, shysters, pimps, prostitutes, farmers, and teenage boys from the surrounding towns headed for the fountain of black gold. Thousands came by special trains from Fort Worth and other parts of

---

*Near Ranger, T&P manager W. K. Gordon, drilling test holes for coal, discovered the Strawn oil pool in 1915. On October 21, 1917, a crew hit a wildcat on the J. H. McClesky property that flowed seventeen hundred barrels a day (Hardman, *Fire*, pp. 132–133; Webb, *Handbook of Texas*, II, 439).—Ed.

Texas. Hundreds of trainloads of pipe, well casings, and drilling and oil-field equipment passed through Mingus for the booming oil field. Long lines of oil tanker cars started moving east. In no time, workers were laying pipelines from Ranger in every direction, with tank farms and pump stations at thirty-mile intervals. Farmers hauled pipe in their wagons at fantastic rates, making more in one day than they could all summer by peddling peaches in Thurber and Mingus. Men and boys who had no teams joined the labor gangs digging ditches and covering pipe. Teenage boys earned an unheard-of five dollars per day, more than they could earn in a month by selling chicken sandwiches to hungry train passengers at Mingus.

Railroad business increased to the point that the T&P installed train dispatchers in Mingus to speed the operation between Fort Worth and Baird. The local carshops worked overtime building new cars and repairing old ones. As the number of trains increased, the T&P demanded more coal from the Thurber mines. The eating houses and drugstore in Mingus did a booming business, and there were no vacant houses or business structures in town. Local doctors were busy day and night, dealing with accidents in the new oil field.

The demand for coal ran high during the war years. Thousands of homes, stores, hotels, and office buildings bought coal for heating. Coal gas was manufactured by many local companies for distribution and sale to residents and firms. Natural gas posed no threat as a source of power. The Lone Star Gas Company was a six-year-old stripling with a limited territory. Power plants depended on coal for generating electricity. When World War I ended in the fall of 1918, few residents in Mingus and Thurber would believe that oil could pose a threat to coal production in their district.

In 1919 the first oil-burning locomotives reached Mingus, and by the end of the year the T&P had abandoned the old coal burners. Coal and railroad company officials doubtless knew that substituting oil for coal would adversely affect the future of Thurber and Mingus. However, the mine and railroad workers expressed no alarm over the switch.

Changes began to take place in Mingus. The T&P dismantled its coal chutes and built steel tanks to supply oil for locomotive tenders. Tank cars soon stood on the railroad sidings instead of coal cars, and three pumpers, one for each eight-hour shift, replaced chute workers at each station. As there was no ash or cinder accumulation from burning oil, the T&P discharged the fire knockers who had cleaned the fireboxes of the locomotives. Hundreds of unskilled laborers who, shovelful by shovelful, had cleared cinders from the roadbed were dismissed. Huge coal-burning moguls pulling long trains had required stokers to shovel a steady stream of coal into the maws of the insatiable fireboxes. But stokers vanished from the scene. One fireman, by manipulating a fuel valve, could regulate the flow of oil to the burners of the largest locomotives. Considering the overall labor costs of operating a railroad, these changes seemed to be minor. Housewives who had fought the battle of cinders and smut on wash-day welcomed the oil burners. They belched no cinders and very little soot from their smokestacks.

Optimism reigned in Thurber and Mingus through 1919. Freight and passenger traffic continued to be heavy on the railroad, and the Texas & Pacific Mercantile and Manufacturing Company of Thurber, a subsidiary of the T&P Coal and Oil Company, closed the second decade with a report of the largest sales in its history. With the coal and oil company rolling in millions, Thurber and Mingus saw long years of steady employment ahead.

But the local economic picture changed drastically in 1921. For the first time in the twentieth century, the T&P Mercantile and Manufacturing Company reported a net loss. The loss was substantial, amounting to roughly 12 percent of gross sales in 1920. Why the sudden reverse? Why did the mercantile and manufacturing company suddenly become a losing operation after more than two decades of reaping annual profits that had ranged up to 25 percent on gross sales? A series of decisions by T&P officials was largely responsible for this situation.

On May 1, 1921, the T&P suddenly shut down the Thurber mines.* Company management blamed the stoppage on a strike by the United Mine Workers locals. The miners labeled the closing a lockout by T&P management. An ominous air settled over the two towns.

With the Ranger discovery, company directors had secured a new charter and changed the name of the corporation to the Texas & Pacific Coal and Oil Company. It had increased its capitalization seventy-fivefold and secured oil leases to thousands of acres of land. Furthermore, shortly after tapping the new field, the company had placed orders for nearly ten million dollars' worth of drilling equip-

---

*In 1921, with its Thurber coal mines operating part-time, the T&P Coal and Oil Company canceled its contract with the UMW, offering reduced pay to those who wished to work. When the two locals went on strike, the company closed the mines (Gentry, "Thurber," pp. 40–41, 103, 122; Hardman, *Fire*, pp. 57–58). The *Fort Worth Star-Telegram* (December 16, 1973) published the recollections of labor leader Lawrence Santi.—Ed.

ment, which was many times its investment in Thurber and its fourteen regularly worked coal mines. In the eyes of the company directors, oil had taken the place of coal.

The appearance of oil-burning locomotives on the T&P tracks
boldly announced a technological change that immediately cut the
need for Thurber coal. Faced with a declining market and falling
prices, the T&P had no alternative but to reduce the operating costs
of its mines. The quickest way to lower costs was to reduce wages, or
so the company claimed.

The decision to scale down wages brought the company into colli-
sion with union locals. The labor agreement between the two parties
had something like another year to run. There was little or no legis-
lation, state or national, governing labor disputes, other than a relatively vague statement in the Clayton Antitrust Act. Every labor dispute, whether over wages, working conditions, or both, had to be
resolved by a slugfest.

There was no bargaining. The T&P announced that it would keep
the mines open if the men would accept a wage reduction of $2.50
per day. This would move wages back to near pre–World War I levels.
Union management knew the mines would be closed unless production costs were lowered, but it refused to accept the deep pay cut. It
suggested a wage reduction of $1.50 per day. The company stood
firm, and the two sides became hopelessly deadlocked. A work
stoppage (strike or lockout) began on May 1, 1921, and the mines
closed down.

Idled men and their families resided in company houses rent free
for several months as the deadlock over wages dragged on. Ultimately, the company decided that it would not reopen the mines and
notified the men to move by a certain date or begin paying rent.
Without jobs, most of the miners in Thurber could not pay rent. An
exodus began.

The UMW reacted immediately. It reportedly had a larger member-
ship in Thurber than in any other mining community in the United
States, and the members had made substantial contributions to the
union since 1903. UMW president John L. Lewis quickly dispatched
financial and material aid to the miners. Hundreds of army tents,
surplus from World War I, arrived in Mingus by rail and were put up
at Grant Town, just north of Thurber, across the line in Palo Pinto
County. Families evicted from Thurber moved to this tent city, where
the lodgings were free.

In addition, the UMW forwarded thousands of dollars to maintain
the residents of the tent city. At first, officers of the locals handled
the distribution, but Lewis soon sent a representative from the na-

tional headquarters to administer the funds and direct other union affairs. His major function was to maintain morale in the camp.

Paggini (I never knew his first name) was Lewis's agent. He was an able administrator with an outstanding personality. He closely monitored the affairs of the strikers and quickly became a member of the Mingus community, taking an active part in lodges, social life, and politics. He possessed a natural friendliness and moved smoothly among the townspeople. Dad was no great admirer of unions, but he both liked and respected Paggini. From my own few contacts with the man, I concluded that he would command the respect of any group with which he might be involved.

Father said that he understood that the UMW monthly check, or checks, totaled $65,000. These payments continued for two years. The bulk of expenditures went for food, but some went for fuel and lights, to replace worn-out clothing, and for medical care of the miners and their families. Dad received, for services rendered, monthly checks for an extended period. These checks varied in size, because he was busier during the winter months when colds and pneumonia were prevalent. There was an exception to this rule: when the strike passed the nine-month point, there was a sharp increase in the doctor's O.B. patients.

At $65,000 per month, the UMW strike fund for Thurber approximated $800,000 a year. The work stoppage at Thurber began in the midst of the first serious post–World War I recession, when there were labor disputes and strikes in coal-mining areas across the country. Under such circumstances, millions of dollars in strike funds were quickly dissipated. A careful study of the Thurber stoppage should have convinced the UMW that there was no chance of reopening the mines there. Paggini soon realized this. He knew that the men were not facing the Texas & Pacific Coal Company; they were battling the Texas & Pacific Coal and *Oil* Company. In this company, coal had become a waif, a stepchild. Profits from the mines, even if reopened, would have been insignificant in comparison to those derived from oil.

As the strike dragged on month after month, the population in the tent city began to decrease. Many realized that they were fighting a lost cause and found employment in the oil fields. This was especially true of men who could pose as craftsmen. Some moved on to semiskilled or unskilled jobs. Still others decided that bootlegging chock beer and moonshine whiskey offered better pay and steadier employment than coal mining or other types of work. A small group joined the ranks of the entrepreneurs as grocers or self-employed truckers. Company doctors had never been part of the tent city, but most of them were no longer needed. One or two located in neighboring towns, but a majority migrated to Fort Worth.

Even with the passage of months, the tent city was still a populous place when the UMW finally concluded that the Thurber mines would not be reopened. Through Paggini, it initiated a resettlement or relocation program. Two hundred Mexicans wished to return to Mexico and did so at the expense of the union. Several hundred others chose to relocate in other states, where they had friends or relatives working in mines. With such ties, their chances of jobs, they felt, should be excellent. The UMW was doubtless pleased with such decisions, because the Thurber miners would again become dues-paying union members. It paid coach fares to places of their choice.

There had been a steady migration of European workers to and from Thurber, especially Italians, in previous years. Many had come and stayed long enough to accumulate what in Italy would be a substantial nest egg, and then returned to the "Old Country." Closing the mines provided an incentive for those planning to leave the United States to depart immediately for their European homelands.

With the residents of the tent city leaving, it soon became a shell of its former self. John L. Lewis finally recalled Paggini and stopped the flow of money from the UMW strike fund. Remaining tents were struck, folded, and carted away. Thurber's era as a coal mining community had ended.

Independently owned mines at neighboring Strawn and Lyra (Mineral City) remained in operation. I do not know when the Strawn mine closed, but Lyra was kept open, during its last several years on a two- or three-day work week, until the summer of 1945 or 1946. However, the Lyra and Strawn mines, although only four and five miles from Mingus, respectively, added little to its local business.

One Thurber miner even tried to run a private mine. He located a vein twenty feet below the surface in Grant Town, sank a shaft, and erected a windlass for raising the mined coal to the surface. After a few years, however, he gave up, ending coal mining in the immediate vicinity of Thurber.

Although a majority of the miners and their families were gone, and trains no longer shuttled coal to the T&P main line at Mingus, Thurber was far from being a ghost town. True, it had hundreds of vacant cottages—houses haunted by the sounds of revelry, music, dancing, kitchen aromas, and the languages of twenty different nationalities. An imaginative ear might still hear the tinkle of glasses and sounds of drinking songs floating from arbors once covered with morning glories. But the company had a formula for eradicating haunts. It removed the homes.

Of the several hundred employees allowed to occupy company houses, a majority worked in the brick plant, which continued to do a flourishing business. Others worked in downtown Thurber, as company stores and the picture show remained open. Smoke poured from the stack at the power plant, and the ice business found ready customers. The T&P maintained its general field offices, which included a large managerial and clerical staff, in Thurber, even though the executive offices were in Fort Worth. A large supply of pipe and other oil-field equipment was kept in the yards at Thurber. Local schools continued to operate, and the annual golf tournament was held as usual. The printshop turned out job work for the company and published the *Thurber Journal* each week, although in a modified form. The U.S. mail continued to serve Thurber through its post office.

The company even erected a cotton gin. A gin operating in Thurber between 1900 and 1920 would have been a sound investment, but it quickly became a money losing venture for the company. Despite the efforts of its manager, Bill Rigsby, an experienced gin man, it faced major problems. By the early 1920s, an agricultural boom hit the high plains, and cotton production shifted from the black land country to the counties around Lubbock. Cotton growing around Thurber slumped.

Although salaries remained healthy, the T&P scaled down its social activities (some said they were more lavish). I cannot recall a big July 4 or a Labor Day picnic in Thurber after the mines shut down in 1921. The Sunday evening band concerts ended. Dan Rafael, a former band member, kept a group going in Mingus for a number of years, and the town even erected a bandstand on a vacant lot south of the railroad. But Dan finally left town to open a steak house in Mineral Wells, and that ended band music for Mingus.

Mingus merchants felt the impact of the mine shutdown much more than the company stores in Thurber did. Several of them, like Joe Abraham, lost up to 50 percent of their trade. In addition, work in the local carshops, which depended almost entirely on Thurber coal shipments, was drastically reduced. The T&P removed its switch engines from the yards, leaving one in use as long as the brick plant ran.

Railroad passenger traffic at Mingus began shrinking. The ticket agent formerly had sold $100,000 in tickets a month for the eastbound Sunshine Special, but his total monthly sales for both east and westbound trains now fell far short of the figure. Payrolls at the depot declined, as freight, express, and passenger business in Mingus produced smaller commissions. Dad lost a number of his patients in the exodus, and his prescription business at the drugstore dropped sharply.

Coal was the only reason why Thurber and Mingus appeared on the map of Texas—and coal was the principal cause for their economic decline. Both communities had relied solely on one resource for their existence, and it proved to be a tenuous thread of life. Although many former boomtowns in the West died when local veins, lodes, or creek beds were worked out, this was not the case with the Thurber-Mingus district. The coal deposits were never depleted. In fact, geologists estimated that 150 million tons of coal lay untouched around Thurber. At the average removal rate of 3,000 tons per workday, it would take 150 years to exhaust these deposits. Technological progress, plus industrial changes, destroyed Thurber coal as a resource. When the Texas & Pacific Railway Company decided that oil was a cheaper, more efficient fuel for its locomotives than coal, and that its use would greatly reduce operating costs, it set the stage for the decline of both towns.

14.   The End of an Era

ON JULY 1, 1922, just fourteen months to the day from the mine closing, the Thurber-Mingus district suffered a second blow. The shop craftsmen in the Mingus railroad yards walked off their jobs. This strike was part of a national work stoppage caused by a dispute between the major railroads and the shop craftsmen's union.* Railroad employees had enjoyed preferential treatment by the Wilson administration during World War I, but from the time the government returned the railroads to private ownership after the war ended, there were signs and rumors of a pending conflict between the roads and their employees. Although I was attending the University of Texas at the time, I kept up with events through letters, newspapers, and summer visits. The walkout in Mingus, followed by the subsequent dismantling of Thurber, virtually destroyed the world I had known as a boy.

The year 1922 opened with newspapers across the country announcing that one hundred major railroads planned to reduce the annual wages of their employees by a total of $125 million. Wages of 400,000 shop craftsmen would be cut by $60 million. Representatives and national officers of the craftsmen's union began negotiations in early spring and continued them through June.

In addition to pay cuts, the railroads wanted to modify certain rules. Their major proposal was to eliminate time-and-a-half pay for overtime and install a piece-work pay base. The union's answer to this was a stubborn no—and the charge that the railroads would be violating the Transportation Act of 1920 by implementing such changes. They also accused the railroads of contracting shopwork to outside firms. With neither side willing to budge, negotiations collapsed. Union officials instructed locals to walk off their jobs at mid-

---

*The national plight of the railway shopmen in 1922 is discussed in Foster Rhea Dulles, *Labor in America*, pp. 239–240.—Ed.

morning on July 1, 1922. In Texas the walkout was virtually 100 percent.

All union men in Mingus, about 140, joined the strike. T&P trains kept moving because the brotherhoods of trainmen refused to honor the picket lines. When strikers in Fort Worth and Mingus ignored a T&P edict to return to work, tempers and violence flared. Mr. Knightlinger,* superintendent of the T&P's Rio Grande Division (Fort Worth to El Paso), stated in the *Fort Worth Record* of July 6 that the company planned to hire strikebreakers in Fort Worth and warned former employees against trespassing on railroad property. This was like waving a red flag before the strikers.

For several years, Knightlinger had frequently visited Mingus in his private car, and he and Dad became good friends. (Dad called the superintendent's small coach a "cracker box.") As long as the walkout lasted, Knightlinger parked his car on a Mingus siding for an overnight stay and slept at our house. Through their conversations, we kept up with developments. On July 7 the *Record* reported that trouble had erupted in Fort Worth between strikers and scabs. Violence quickly spread to other Texas railroad centers. The Missouri, Kansas & Texas Railroad requested Gov. Pat Neff to send National Guard units to Denison to protect its properties, and the T&P added its request for guard units on July 12. Neff ignored these requests. He was seeking renomination in the Democratic primary, which was two or three weeks away, and knew that calling out the guard at the behest of railroads would place him in political jeopardy.

Texas railroads sought help elsewhere. They secured an order from a federal judge on July 10 for the commissioning of twenty-five deputy U.S. marshals to guard their properties. In those days, the presence of a marshal, or a deputy marshal, was considered to be as awesome as having a Texas Ranger on hand to prevent or quell a riot. One of the deputies was sent to Mingus.

A few days after the new deputy arrived, Dad was awakened about midnight by pistol shots near the railroad tracks. He dressed hurriedly and went out in the darkness to see what had happened. A small group of men had gathered near the tracks where the deputy lay on the ground mortally wounded. He had been ambushed by an assailant firing through the small triangle formed by two car wheels sitting on a steel rail. According to Dad, the deputy had fired back, his bullets splattering both wheels, but he missed the center of the triangle. The killer had fled into the night. No one saw him leave, or

---

*Jesse W. Knightlinger, in *Fort Worth City Directory* (1922). Information courtesy Fort Worth Public Library.—Ed.

had an idea which way he had gone. No one was ever apprehended. Dad was positive he could name the killer, while the yard clerk said he would bet on one of two names. No court would have considered their opinions as circumstantial evidence. Dad was given the deputy's pistol. In another case at Mingus, a strikebreaker was severely stomped and beaten at the picture show one night by sympathizers of the striking shopmen.

The history of Mingus would have ended suddenly if one striker had carried out his plan. Somehow he had managed to obtain five quarts of nitroglycerin, and rumor had it that he intended to blow up the Mingus carshops. Deputy sheriff Bob Loflin lost no time in contacting his friend. He asked him if he knew that five quarts of nitro, because of the flatness of the country, would blow Mingus off the map and kill everybody in the place. Getting more specific, Loflin asked if he had considered that he and his wife, Ed Merritt and his wife, Pete Tarmino, Doc, and many others would be blown to bits. No, the man did not want to kill anybody. If that was true, Loflin told him to get rid of the nitro and to forget the matter. The yards and Mingus remained intact and nothing more was done about the threat. Loflin admitted he had seen no explosives, but wanted to put an end to the rumor.

Unlike the striking coal miners in Thurber, no railroad man on strike suffered an immediate dislocation in his homelife. The shop-workers owned their homes and probably received assistance from the union strike fund. Also, they possibly had more savings on hand when their strike began than the average Thurber miner did. The Mingus shopmen ignored the fact that their jobs were doomed. They assumed that the need to service and repair railroad rolling stock would halt the movement of trains. They scrutinized every passing train, listening for the bumping of flattened car wheels and looking for signs of heated axles, loosened drawbars, or other indications of impending trouble for the railroad.

All of these men were friends of my parents. Some were croquet players and the strike gave them free evenings for games. When a train passed with a bumpy wheel or flames dancing from an axle hotbox, the striker would interrupt the game with a fit of boisterous laughter and predict, "It won't be long now before the old T P will be begging us to come back to work." That day never came. With the Thurber mines closed, the railroad shops and yards at Mingus became surplus property—and the workers there became surplus labor.

The strike dragged on and the shop craftsmen ultimately lost. Few railroads recalled former employees. At Mingus, Nath Cowan was the only striker to be rehired by the T&P, and only five or six found employment with other railroads. None got work on a major line. As the shopmen at Mingus were trained in carpentry and other crafts, there was no sudden exodus because they had lost their jobs. A number sought nonrailroad work, eventually scattering to growing towns throughout the Southwest. Those who left Mingus frequently sold their homes to oil-field workers who paid a fraction of their value and moved them to sites near their employment. Some workers had kept family farms and returned to them, rather than fight a competitive job market. Those who considered themselves too old to put down roots elsewhere lived out their years in Mingus.

With the drop in freight and passenger business at Mingus, the railroads reduced the number of employees at the depot. Most of them had built up considerable seniority and therefore bumped younger men from jobs at other stations along the T&P. This was also true of switch engine crews that were transferred from Mingus to Fort Worth, Dallas, Big Spring, and El Paso. The total loss of jobs in Mingus involved heads of 140 households, which was a heavy blow to a town of two thousand population. Fortunately, the emigration went slowly, and it was several years before empty houses became noticeable in Mingus.

Although it closed its coal mines in 1921, the Texas & Pacific Coal and Oil Company kept its Thurber brick plant running through the 1920s, furnishing quality brick for various purposes. Highway construction was booming. The Texas State Highway Department had been created in 1917,* and Good Roads groups sprang up in well-populated counties to discuss plans to link 256,000 square miles of the state with a network of paved roads. A larger dream was the Bankhead Highway (later U.S. 80), which would cross the nation by way of the Southern states, Texas, New Mexico, and Arizona to California.

As Thurber vitrified paving brick had lifted many city streets out of the mud, the State of Texas considered it for use on state roads. At the behest of Gov. James E. Ferguson, the Highway Department ran an experiment on the road between Belton and Temple. Engineers selected a test section and laid an outside binding of asphalt, then a strip of brick about eighteen inches in width, a wider ribbon of asphalt, another strip of brick, and a final ribbon of asphalt. The brick provided running surfaces for car wheels. The experiment showed that asphalt paving on either side of the brick rose like small hills

---

*Support for Texas roads and highways shifted from the counties to the state in 1917 and increasingly included federal monies (Richardson et al., *Texas*, pp. 350–351).—Ed.

and in wet weather became extremely slick, making traction difficult. Brick highways were the best. Contractors purchased hundreds of thousands of Thurber bricks for the state highway system.

When the Great Depression broke in the fall of 1929, the demand for brick fell sharply. The following year the Thurber brick plant closed down, and several hundred men lost their jobs. Since no labor dispute had been involved at the plant, the Texas & Pacific Coal and Oil Company performed a remarkable act of paternalism. It allowed the idled plant men to remain in their company houses rent free and to receive thirty dollars' credit in the company store each month. This apparently continued for several years.*

When the Thurber brick plant closed, Mingus was already in decline. The volume of freight had fallen, and the Texas & Pacific removed its last switch engine and transferred its yardmaster and yard clerk to Fort Worth. The freight clerk went to Dallas. At least four years earlier, Mitt Doss had closed the Baxendale drugstore in Mingus and moved his stock and fixtures to Colorado City. My younger brother, Harry, graduated from the Baylor School of Pharmacy in 1924 and returned home to serve as Dad's pharmacist. He faced a bleak future. The lunchrooms that had served train crews and travelers started closing, until only one remained. John Osborn burned to death in 1928, and his brother closed his grocery store. The Ferd Hill grocery had long since shut its doors. One by one, residents and firms moved away from Mingus until by 1930 it was in worse shape than Thurber.

During the 1930s, Mingus tried desperately to lift itself by its economic bootstraps. It finally incorporated and elected a mayor and city council. The city fathers petitioned for Public Works Administration funds to tap into the Thurber water system and lay water mains in Mingus, complete with fire hydrants on alternate corners. They even bought a second-hand fire truck of ancient vintage, which sat around in the old Loflin garage until its tires rotted off. Mart Smith, who refused to sell land for a Lone Star gas plant, and the character who refused to let Eastman Kodak have a spot of land, fairly well guaranteed a desolate future for Mingus. Eventually Mingus lost its public school affiliation and the few scholastics began riding buses to Gordon. This happened even though federal funds had constructed a school gymnasium. The building was later razed, there being no effort to preserve it as a community center.

---

*My uncle, L. B. Gibson, who had worked at the brick plant for many years and lived between the plant and Thurber's Big Lake, remained in a company house until 1934, when he settled on a farm in the vicinity.

Seventeen years after it became a major corporation, the Texas & Pacific Coal and Oil Company suddenly moved (1934) its general offices to Fort Worth and started leveling Thurber to the ground. Local rumors said that T&P directors ordered the move to get rid of lingering vestiges of unionism. But unionism in the United States was at its nadir during the early 1930s. In my view, the reason for the transfer was quite different. Small-town men with small-town wives had gained high positions in the company, and being big shots, their headquarters for field operations should be in a big city like Fort Worth. (At that time, Fort Worth loomed larger than New York in the eyes of many adult Texans with small-town backgrounds.) I recall seeing some of the highest standing around the depot in Mingus waiting for the eastbound Sunshine Special, looking right through old friends, never deigning to speak to them or evincing the slightest sign of recognition. I submit that a major reason for moving the general offices from Thurber was to satisfy the personal whims of some high company officials.

The reduction of Thurber was ruthless.* The company ordered everything on the surface to be torn down or dug up. Office buildings, stores, opera house, clubhouse, school buildings, churches, post office, residences (brick and frame), brick plant, ice and power plant, and cotton gin were offered for sale. Rails, ties, mining machinery, power lines, pipe, anything and everything—all were to be removed. Three-fourths of the tall water standpipe reservoir on a hill bordering the town was taken down. The Catholic church building was moved to Mingus. The T&P even determined the closing date of the U.S. Post Office at Thurber.

A few things escaped the wrecking crews. At the request of Superintendent W. K. Gordon, the old brick smokestack that served the power and ice plant was left standing. Gordon's home was not touched and served for years as a weekend retreat for company officials. The home of the assistant superintendent, a large store building, and the drugstore also were left standing. The store became the annual reunion site for former Thurber residents, and the drugstore was converted into a filling station and hamburger joint.

As Thurber was being erased from the map, Mingus slipped further toward oblivion. The spur track connecting Thurber to the T&P's main line in Mingus was taken up, and the right-of-way and

---

*The dismantling of Thurber (with photographs) is described by Willie M. Floyd, "Thurber, Texas: An Abandoned Coal Field Town" (M.A. thesis, Southern Methodist University, 1939).

land occupied by the car yards were fenced in for a pasture. John Hickman quit peddling Thurber ice to Mingus customers, as electric iceboxes were appearing in every household. The Bradley family gave up the telephone exchange, and the Southwestern Bell Telephone System took charge. Passenger trains, east- or westbound, no longer stopped. Shorty Bradley took the outgoing mail to the depot in his truck and brought the sacks of incoming mail tossed from the train back to the post office. Thurber, or what was left of it, was served by a rural route out of Mingus.

After Thurber disappeared, freight trains from Fort Worth no longer stopped in Mingus, but passed straight through to Baird. Eastbound trains stopped at Baird, then went on directly to Fort Worth. But the Thurber shutdown was not wholly responsible for changing the freight schedule. The oil fields around Ranger, Eastland, and Cisco were no longer booming, and local traffic was light.

When the T&P company offices were moved to Fort Worth, Dad lost those patients who had stayed in Thurber to the last. After thirty years in Mingus, his practice sank to an all-time low. He looked over a number of West Texas towns and in 1938 decided to try Iraan in the Yates oil field. He kept his home and office in Mingus, but bought a building in Iraan to serve as both residence and office. He did well in the new field because a number of former Thurberites lived there. But after five or six years in Iraan, Dad contracted pernicious anemia and returned to Mingus. World War II was under way, and doctors were a scarce commodity in both Palo Pinto and Erath counties, so he did exceedingly well during the war years.

For years, old-timers would speculate about the fate of Thurber. From the time the T&P closed the mines, the future of the town had rested solely in the hands of the company directors. Thurber could have remained a town of five thousand inhabitants or more for many years, had those men willed it. The brick plant would have faced lean years during the 1930s, but would have recovered. Several hundred men worked at the plant, and this in itself would have ensured a modest-sized town. Mingus would have shrunk to one thousand people, about half of its former size, but the Thurber employees living there would have remained as long as there were company jobs. Thurber was about seventy miles (a respectable distance) from company executive offices in Fort Worth, and the T&P had invested considerable money in providing its employees with every facility for modern living. Operating costs were low because it owned the office buildings, power and ice plant, water system, entertainment centers, service yards, and fuel supplies. It paid county and state taxes on these properties, but no local taxes, either city or school. The company also maintained its general offices and supply headquarters for its oil-field operations in Thurber.

Mingus provided service to the T&P railroad until after World War II. Then as diesel-electric locomotives replaced the oil burners, the railroad closed the pump station, discharged the three men who had tended the water facilities, and dismantled the oil storage tank. The diesels did not require fuel and water every fifty miles or so. With the close of the war, freight and passenger service to and from Mingus ended. After fifty years' service, the T&P railroad wrecked the brick depot to save on state, county, city, and school taxes.

Today, freight trains roll through Mingus on a regular schedule without stopping. No one remembers that at one time this division point furnished the Texas & Pacific Railway more revenue than any other station west of Fort Worth. Now and then a freight may stop on the long passing track to permit another train to go by. Otherwise Mingus, with only a tenth of its 1920 population, is nothing more than a small cluster of buildings scattered along the main line.

My boyhood years in the Thurber-Mingus coal district provided instructive and rewarding experiences. I was fortunate to see two ways of life—the old and the new—grapple with everyday problems and human concerns. From my window on the world, I was fascinated by the passing scene, the tempo of change, and the interaction of family and society. Life in Mingus and Thurber furnished both lessons and insights that shaped attitudes, appreciation, and love of family. I hope these memories will rescue part of that world for posterity.

References

Unpublished

Floyd, Willie M. "Thurber, Texas: An Abandoned Coal Field Town." M.A. thesis, Southern Methodist University, 1939.

Gentry, Mary Jane. "Thurber, Life and Death of a Texas Town." M.A. thesis, University of Texas, 1946.

John S. Spratt, Sr. Collection. In possession of John S. Spratt, Jr., Louisville, Kentucky.

Published

Allen, Ruth. *Chapters in the History of Organized Labor in Texas.* Austin: University of Texas Publication 4143, 1941.

Bate, W. N. *Frontier Legend: Texas Finale of Capt. William F. Drannan, Pseudo Frontier Comrade of Kit Carson.* New Bern, N.C.: Owen G. Dunn Company, 1954.

Bielinski, Leo S. "Beer, Booze, Bootlegging and Bocci Ball in Thurber-Mingus." *West Texas Historical Association Year Book* 59 (1983): 75–89.

Browning, David. "The Price of Progress: The Story of Thurber's Fate." *Texas Historian* 31 (September 1970): 24–29.

Bush, I. J. *Gringo Doctor.* Caldwell, Id.: Caxton Printer, 1939.

Cravens, John N. "Two Miners and Their Families in the Thurber-Strawn Coal Mines, 1905–1918." *West Texas Historical Association Year Book* 45 (1969): 115–126.

Dulles, Foster Rhea. *Labor in America.* New York: Thomas Y. Crowell Company, 1960.

Faulkner, Harold U. *American Economic History.* 7th ed. New York: Harper & Brothers, 1954.

Fine Art Reproductions of Old & Modern Masters. New York: New York Graphic Society, 1980.

Gooch, Gordon. "Mingus, the Pittsburgh of Texas." *Junior Historian* 13 (May 1953): 6.

Hardman, Weldon B. *Fire in a Hole.* Stephenville, Tex.: Thurber Historical Association, 1975.

"Henrietta (Hetty) Robinson Green." In *National Cyclopaedia of American Biography*. 62 vols. New York: James T. White & Company, 1898–1984, XV, 128.

Hooks, Michael Q. "Thurber: A Unique Texas Community." *Panhandle-Plains Historical Review* 56 (1983): 1–17.

Hughes, Alton. *Pecos: A History of the Pioneer West*. Seagraves, Tex.: Pioneer Book Publishers, 1978.

Hughes, Stella. *Chuck Wagon Cookin'*. Tucson: University of Arizona Press, 1974.

Knight, Oliver. *Fort Worth: Outpost on the Trinity*. Norman: University of Oklahoma Press, 1953.

Lee, Guy Carleton, ed. *The World's Orators* . . . 10 vols. New York: G. P. Putnam's Sons, 1900.

McLean, William Hunter, comp. *From Ayer to Thurber: Three Hunter Brothers and the Winning of the West*. Fort Worth, Tex.: News Printing Company, 1978.

Malvern, Gladys. *Valiant Minstrel: The Story of Sir Harry Lauder*. New York: Julian Messner, 1943.

Maroney, James C. "The Unionization of Thurber, 1903." *Red River Valley Historical Review* 4 (Spring 1979): 27–32.

Paddock, Buckley B. *History of Texas: Fort Worth and the Texas Northwest Edition*. 4 vols. Chicago: Lewis Publishing Company, 1922.

Reed, S. G. *A History of Texas Railroads* . . . 2d ed. Houston, Tex.: St. Clair Publishing Company, 1941.

Reinhold, Ruth M. *Sky Pioneering*. Tucson: University of Arizona Press, 1982.

Richardson, Rupert N., et al. *Texas: The Lone Star State*. 3d ed. Englewood Cliffs, N.J.: Prentice-Hall, 1970.

Spratt, John S. *The Road to Spindletop: Economic Change in Texas, 1875–1901*. Dallas, Tex.: Southern Methodist University Press, 1955.

———. "When Bob Threw Christmas Away." *Southwest Review* 53 (Winter 1968): 86–91.

Vandiver, Frank E. *Black Jack: The Life and Times of John J. Pershing*. 2 vols. College Station: Texas A&M University Press, 1977.

Webb, Walter P., ed. *Handbook of Texas*. 2 vols. Austin: Texas State Historical Association, 1952.

Index

Iko (carnival freak), 51
Iraan, Tex., 127
Italian Hill, xiv, 93

James, Cowan & Nolton Company,
xii
James, Jesse, 22, 38
Jester, Lew, 68–69
Johnson, Harvey, xii
Johnson, Mary Rebecca, 56n
Johnson, William W., xii, xiii
Juárez, Mex., 22

Kern, John, xxii, 47–48
Kern, Mrs. ———— (Mingus resi-
dent), 88
Knightlinger, Jesse W., 122
Knights of Labor, xii, xiii, 6–7

*Ladies Almanac and Weather
Guide*, 86
Lewis, John L., 116–118
Liberty Bonds (World War I): 106,
112–113
Lingleville, Tex., 1
Link, Oma, 113
Loflin, Bob, 22, 48, 66, 68, 123, 125
Loflin Mercantile Company, 7, 66
Lone Star Gas Company, 114, 125
Loving County, Tex., 91
Lucas oil gusher, xvii
Lubbock, Tex., 119
Luigi (Mingus artist), 45–46
Lynn, Peggy, 48
Lyra, Tex., xiv, 29n, 47, 118

Magnolia Petroleum Company, 66,
104
Marshall, Mutt, 50
Marshall, Tex., 30
Marston, Edgar L., xiii, xiv
Matheson, ———— (Mingus
gambler), 34
Mentone, Tex., 91
Merritt, Ed, 123
Methodists: in Mingus, 15, 41, 42,
91, 99

Mexican Revolution, 104
Mexicans, 2, 6, 11, 118
Midland, Tex., 24, 91
Mineral City. *See* Lyra, Tex.
Mineral Wells, Tex., 71, 119; fairs
at, 66, 90
Mingus, Tex.: airplane in, 50; autos
in, xxii, 10–11, 47–48, 68, 74;
bandstand in, 119; banking in, 8,
14, 56–58; barter in, xxii, 56;
blacksmith in, 7, 74; brewery in,
8; buildings in, 8–9; burros in,
29; businesses in, 7–8, 58–60,
62–66, 68–70, 75, 125; butcher
in, 68; carshops in, xxi, 6, 20,
31, 47, 102, 110, 114, 119, 123;
churches in, 11–12, 15, 33, 37–
38, 41–42, 54, 80, 88, 111; circuses in, 46–47; coal in, xi, xvi,
xxi, 6, 18–20, 22, 30–31, 107,
114, 115; cotton gin in, 74; decline of, 125–128; depot in, xvi,
xxi, 4–6, 11, 21, 23, 30, 77, 107,
120, 124, 126–128; drugstores in,
11, 21, 32, 34, 58–60, 114, 120;
during World War I, 111–113;
electricity in, 11; entertainment
in, 7–8, 36, 45, 53, 119; flu in,
62; funerals in, 66–67; holidays
in, 98, 102; hotel in, 7, 69, 85; ice
in, 12–13; kerosene in, xxii, 5,
11–12, 14, 63, 80, 104; land-
ownership in, 7, 9; lawyers in, 7,
72; liquor in, 5, 9, 11, 15–16,
36–38; livery stable in, 68; lodge
halls in, 11–12, 35–36; lumberyard in, 7, 56, 70–71, 113; mi-
norities in, 11, 14, 27–28, 64, 85;
parties in, 35, 41–43; peddlers in,
64; pool hall in, 11, 36; population of, xvi, 124, 127–128; post
office in, 4, 57, 127; as rail junction, xi, xxi, 4; rail strike in,
121–124; railroad employees in,
4, 31, 109–110, 124; and Ranger
boom, 114–116; restaurants in, 7,
21, 23, 68–69, 114, 125; rural in-

takes speaking course, 91; treats
circus injuries, 47; tries golf, 36;
wins phonograph, 65, 88; and
World War I, 113
Spratt, Mrs. John T. (Martha Louisa
Felts): condemns whiskey, 38, 82;
decorates buggy, 52; dislikes
Mingus, 4–5; handles money, 57;
household chores of, 70, 77–78,
80–85, 88; keeps garden, 81, 86;
makes clothes, 65, 95; makes
soap, 84–85; marries, xvi, 1; pre-
pares holiday dinners, 97–98,
101–102; and sister Callie, 2, 4;
visits Ross Ranch, 91–92
Spratt, M. Tempie: death of, 66–67
Spratt's Cosmetic (hand lotion), 84
Stephenville, Tex., 85
Stephenville Tribune, 39
Story of Cole Younger, 22, 39
Strawn, Tex., xii, 18, 33, 47, 69, 113;
businesses at, 56–57, 66–67;
mines at, xiv, 118; schools at,
xvii, 13
Stump Hill, xiv
Sunshine Special (train), 18, 24,
119, 126
Swift (packing plant), 12

Tarmino, Pete, 123
Teichman, Joe, 58, 73–74
Temple, Tex., 124
Tennessee, 98–99
Texas, University of, xvii, 106, 121
Texas & Pacific Coal and Oil Company: directors of, determine future, 127–128; levels Thurber,
126–127; moves executive
offices, 119; negotiates contract
with T&P Railway, xiii; and 1921
strike, 115–117; organization
of, 75; paternal act of, 125; runs
brick plant, 124–125; runs
cotton gin, 75
Texas & Pacific Coal Company:
changes name, 75, 117; and
Chautauqua, 45; contracts with

T&P Railway, xiii; develops
Ranger oil field, xxii, 31, 104,
111, 113; develops Thurber, xi,
xvi, xxi, 6, 33; hires lawman, 13;
organization of, xiii
Texas & Pacific Mercantile and
Manufacturing Company: oper-
ates company enterprises in
Thurber, xiii, 71, 75, 102, 115;
payroll of, 55, 58; runs stagecoach, 55
Texas & Pacific Railway: adver-
tises special fares, 71; builds
lunch counters, 69; carries mail,
107; carries Thurber payroll, 55;
circus trains on, 46, 108–109;
coal cars on, 18; drummers on,
22; dumps cinders, 11; encoun-
ters floods, 24–25; freight on,
14–15, 30, 103–104; hauls oil-
field equipment, 114; hires deputy marshals, 122–123; influ-
ences towns, xvii, xxi, 25, 107,
109, 114–115; leases boxcars, 3;
length of trains on, xxii, 17, 20;
locomotives of, xi, xxi, xxii, 17–
20, 25, 107, 114–116, 120, 128;
maintenance of, 18; meal stops
of, 21; needs coal, xi–xiii, xxi, 30;
news butch on, 21–22, 39, 91;
passenger trains on, 17, 21; in
Pecos, 2, 91; pollutes air, 20–21,
103; and rail strike, 121–124;
refrigerator cars on, 12–13, 107;
robbed, 55–56; runs special
trains, 106, 108, 113; segregation
on, 22; speed of, xxii, 17–18,
23–24; spur to Coalville, xii;
spur to Thurber, xiii, 126; tank
cars on, 18, 104, 114; trackage on,
17–18, 20, 103; uses coal chutes,
xi, 19, 107; water for, 18, 104;
whistles of, set schedules, 25, 26;
wrecker of, 24. *See also* Cannon
Ball; Sunshine Special
Texas Institute of Letters, xvii
Texas National Guard, 122

Mingus, 62, 73, 105, 111, 114;
  and railroads, 106, 107, 121
World War II, 127–128
Wright, Jeff, 5

Yates Oil Field, 127
Younger, Cole, 22, 38–39

Zack Miller's 101 Ranch Circus, 108